Power Up
Your Mind

Learn faster,
work smarter

Bill Lucas

NICHOLAS BREALEY
PUBLISHING

L O N D O N

First published by
Nicholas Brealey Publishing in 2001
Reprinted (twice) 2002, 2003, 2004

3–5 Spafield Street
Clerkenwell, London
EC1R 4QB, UK
Tel: +44 (0)20 7239 0360
Fax: +44 (0)20 7239 0370

100 City Hall Plaza, Suite 501
Boston
MA 02108, USA
Tel: (888) BREALEY
Fax: (617) 523 3708

www.nbrealey-books.com
www.bill-lucas.com

ISBN 1-85788-275-X

British Library Cataloguing in Publication Data
A catalogue record for this book is available from the British Library.

Library of Congress Cataloging-in-Publication Data
Lucas, Bill.
    Power up your mind : learn faster, work smarter / Bill Lucas.
        p. cm.
    Includes bibliographical references and index.
    ISBN 1-85788-275-X
    1. Learning, Psychology of. 2. Work--Psychological aspects. I. Title.

BF318 .L83 2001
153.1'5--dc21

2001035940

Printed in Finland by WS Bookwell.

Contents

Acknowledgments

T HIS BOOK COULD NOT HAVE BEEN WRITTEN WITHOUT THE LOVING support of my wife, Henrietta, who read every page of the manuscript and helped me to say what I meant, nor without the many practical insights I have gained from my son, Thomas.

I am particularly grateful for all those who have allowed me to interview them in depth: Sir Bob Reid, friend and one of the most experienced business leaders I know; Joyce Taylor, Managing Director of Discovery Networks Europe; Lord Marshall, Chairman of British Airways; Neil Chambers, Director of London's Natural History Museum; Will Hutton, Chief Executive of the Industrial Society, author, and ex-Fleet Street Editor; Hilary Cropper, Chief Executive of the FI Group plc; Chris Mellor, Group Managing Director of Anglian Water; Zoe Van Zwanenberg, Chief Executive of the Scottish Leadership Foundation; Jayne-Anne Gadhia, Managing Director of Virgin One Account; Sir Michael Bichard, Permanent Secretary at the Department for Education and Employment; and Professor Amin Rajan, author, strategist, and Chief Executive of Create.

A number of people kindly read the manuscript and offered me excellent advice: Dr Peter Honey, Managing Director of Peter Honey Learning; John Grant, Co-Founder of St Luke's and now Owner Manager of The John Grant; Maryjo Scrivani and Michael Joseph, Co-Directors of Partners in Learning; Mike Leibling, Director of Trainset and formerly of Saatchi & Saatchi; Mark Watson, Managing Director of Purple Works; and Professor Bob Fryer, Assistant Vice-Chancellor of Southampton University and the chief architect of Britain's strategy for lifelong learning. Toby Greany and Michelle Wake at the Campaign for Learning; Akber Pandor, Head of Learning at KPMG; and Nicholas Brealey and Sue Coll, my excellent publishers, have been particularly helpful with the structure and title of the book and with many useful ideas.

In shaping my thoughts I have benefited enormously from those with whom I have worked and come into contact in the last few years: Simon Greenly, Chairman of the Campaign for Learning; Dr. Javier Bajer, Chief Executive of the Talent Foundation; Professor Guy Claxton, author and thinker about lifelong learning; Arie de Geus, author and management expert; Charles Handy, author and management guru; Tony Buzan, author and Chairman of the Brain Trust; Sir Christopher Ball, Chancellor of Derby University and Founding Patron of the Campaign for Learning; Colin Rose, Managing Director of Accelerated Learning Systems, author, and inspirational thinker; Alistair Smith, inspirational trainer, writer, and Director of Alite; Jim Smith and Andrea Spurling, Co-Directors of Bamford Taggs; Ian Windle, Managing Director of Celemi Ltd; Professor Susan Greenfield, eminent scientist, broadcaster, and author; and all those not mentioned here whose ideas have helped me develop mine.

Most recently, I have been particularly stimulated by a series of seminars held at the Royal Institution and organized by the Lifelong Learning Foundation. If I have made any mistakes in my interpretation of current neuroscience, I hope my new scientific friends will forgive me and help me to correct the errors for subsequent editions.

And finally, thanks go to my amazing team at the Campaign for Learning, who have been a constant source of motivation and inspiration to me for the last four years.

Introduction

THIS BOOK IS BASED ON THE NOTION THAT WE ALL HAVE THE CAPACITY TO succeed, but most of us only use a very small portion of our minds, and therefore of our capacity. In an age when creativity and time are the key commodities, learning how to learn is the key skill and the brain is the key organ. Only if we can learn faster and more effectively will we be able to thrive.

Most of us don't understand the central role our minds have in helping us to perform more effectively: we are simply not taught how to learn or how to apply our learning. While we have discovered more about the brain and how it works in the last decade than we have ever known before, we apply very little of this in our daily working or personal lives.

It is possible for everyone to learn faster, work smarter, and be more fulfilled.

Power Up Your Mind translates what we know about how the brain works into useful insights for the workplace. It has been written from the conviction that intelligence is multifaceted and not fixed at birth. It draws ideas from the broadest possible range of subject areas, from neuroscience to psychology, motivation theory to accelerated learning, memory to diet.

THE 5 RS

Contrary to what you may have been taught at school, being good at the 3Rs—Reading, wRiting, and aRithmetic—will not be enough for you to get very far today. While everyone certainly needs these basic skills, in the era of lifelong learning there are a much broader set of dispositions that we all need to have. These are the 5Rs: Resourcefulness, Remembering, Resilience, Reflectiveness, and Responsiveness. These new skills are explored in Parts II and III of this book.

INTELLIGENCE AND THE MIND

A similarly narrow view has been taken toward the idea of intelligence in the past century. While the word "intelligence" entered the English language in Europe during the early Middle Ages, it has become a synonym for IQ or intellectual quotient. This one kind of intelligence has dominated our experiences of schooling and influenced many of the psychometric tests we undergo and use at work. Invented by Alfred Binet and William Stern at the beginning of the twentieth century, IQ's influence has been pernicious, artificially inflating the importance of language and figures and taking no account of creativity, common sense, or the ability to manage emotions.

Yet, we know now that intelligence involves a combination of "know-how" and "know-what" across a multitude of contexts. If you are intelligent, you are good at using your mind in many different ways. If your mind is working well, you are able to learn to do many things that you did not think you could do. Nurture not nature is in the ascendency.

For most of the time that it has existed as a concept, intelligence has been linked to the brain. Interestingly, the ancient Egyptians believed that a person's ability to think resided in their heart, while their judgment came from either their brain or their kidneys!

One of the most compelling accounts of how the human brain has evolved is contained in Steven Mithen's *The Prehistory of the Mind*. As an archeologist, Mithen charts the development of the brain in pleasingly accessible ways. He describes three clear phases.

From six million to four and a half million years ago, human beings had a smaller brain, about a third of its size today, which was capable only of displaying limited intelligence. It could take simple decisions according to simple rules, for example about food, shelter, and survival.

In the second period, from four and a half million to about 100,000 years ago, much more specific kinds of intelligent activity developed. The beginning of language during this period is an obvious example.

The third period, from 100,000 to about 10,000 years ago, sees the emergence of a much more complex brain and more generalized types of intelligent activity. Key in this last period are the development of culture and religion.

Not surprisingly, scientists have for some time tried to link particular intelligences or attributes to particular parts of the brain. The most famous of these is the idea of phrenology, which grew up in the nineteenth century, originally developed by Franz Gall in Germany. Gall imagined that you could draw a map of the mind and identify different areas, each responsible for a specific aspect of our life.

By the 1920s, famous French psychologist Jean Piaget could say that intelligence is "what you use when you don't know what you want to do."

In the last two decades, we have found out an enormous amount about intelligence. Many books have been published on the subject, some of them becoming bestsellers. They have shown us that there are many different intelligences, not just the one that most of us grew up with, IQ. And in doing so, they have released us all to begin to recognize our potential across all our talents.

Psychologist Howard Gardner, more than anyone, has revolutionized the concept by introducing the idea of there being not one but eight intelligences. Interestingly, he started in the 1980s with seven, introduced an eighth, the naturalist intelligence, in the 1990s, and has recently been toying with a ninth, existential intelligence. Daniel Goleman has explored one area in particular and coined a new phrase, emotional intelligence or EQ. Writers like Charles Handy and Robert Sternberg have pondered the existence of many more than eight intelligences. Recently, Danah Zohar has invented the concept of spiritual intelligence, SQ. John Guilford would have us believe that there are 120 different kinds!

READY, GO, STEADY

At the heart of this book is a model of how we learn—Ready, Go, Steady—which can help you transform the way you perform.

Learning is learnable. Learning to learn is a kind of "learnacy" that we all need to acquire.

There are three important stages to learning to learn, each one of which is explored in a separate part of the book:

Ready

Before you can start learning you need to be in the right emotional state. The environment around you needs to be conducive and, most importantly, you need to have actively switched on your mind.

Go

As you learn you need to be able to use a wide range of different techniques. You need to understand yourself as a learner. You need to be able to know how to release your own creativity. You need staying power, and you need to know how to deal with both success and failure.

Steady

When you have learned something, you need to be able to reflect on it and apply it in your own life, changing and adapting the way you do things accordingly.

POWERING UP YOUR MIND

For far too long, these three key stages have been viewed in isolation when they need to be taken together. If you can do all three things well, then you will truly have powered up your mind.

This book will help you to be ready, to go out and learn with confidence, and to be steady when it comes to putting your learning into practice. It will always come back to some common-sense questions: So what? What do I need to know about this? Does it work? How can I apply it in my life? How will it help me to be more successful at work and in my personal life?

To help you see how this can be applied, I have included direct personal observations from a number of business leaders whom I interviewed specially for this book. These men and women, from a wide variety of sectors, are already leading their organizations in ways that clearly seek to get the best out of their people's minds.

There are also activities, facts, questions, quotations, pictures, and a range of other stimuli to engage you in an active dialog.

You do not need to be a brain scientist or a lover of business books to enjoy, understand, and apply these ideas. Neither do you have to become a disciple of any one philosophy to reap benefit from the insights contained here. *Power Up Your Mind* is a user's guide for busy business people to the way their minds work. You will find in it a brief description of the most important techniques and the key research findings that will enable you to be smarter in the way you work and live. You will also find original thoughts and ideas that appear nowhere else.

Putting some of these simple suggestions into practice will help you realize your potential and achieve the personal success that you deserve. Sometimes it may be helpful to rely on your instincts and just try things, rather than getting bogged down in explanations. "Why," as the Dodo said in *Alice's Adventures in Wonderland*, "the best way to explain it is to do it."

Part I

Get Ready to Learn

Going beneath the surface

COMING UP IN THIS PART

◆   A guided tour of your brain
◆   How to look after your brain
◆   How to be emotionally ready to learn
◆   How to motivate yourself to learn
◆   How to create a good learning environment
◆   How to overcome barriers to learning

PART I LOOKS LIKE THIS

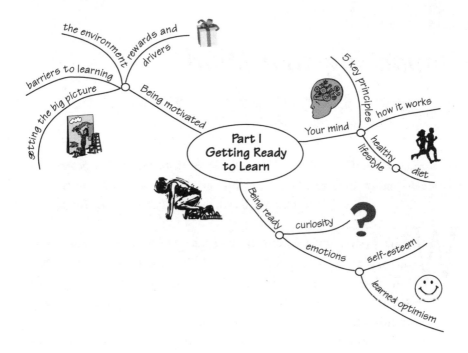

A KEY SENTENCE TO REMEMBER FROM THIS S   'ON

When it comes to our mind, most of us know l   'bout it than we do about the engine of our car.

A FAMOUS THOUGHT TO CONSIDER

Life is like a ten speed bicycle: most of us have gears we never use.

Charles M Schulz

1

Unpacking Your Mind

No one would think of lighting a fire today by rubbing two sticks together. Yet much of what passes for education is based on equally outdated concepts.
Gordon Dryden, *The Learning Revolution*

W E ALL GO TO SCHOOL, WHERE WE LEARN SUBJECTS LIKE SCIENCE AND history. We also develop various skills, mostly related to subjects but also some life skills. Strangely, however, very few people I meet have ever been taught *how* to learn. We talk about literacy and numeracy—but what about "learnacy"?

When I talk to audiences I ask them which they think is the most important part of their body when it comes to learning. Not surprisingly, they point to their heads. I then ask them how much time they spent at school or college or business school learning about their minds and there is an embarrassed and, increasingly these days, a worried silence. People are beginning to understand the real importance of the concept of learnacy, first talked about by Guy Claxton a few years ago.

The situation is similar across organizations of all kinds. There is much talk of global marketplaces, performance, cost cutting, knowledge management, culture, values, leadership development, and so on. But in most cases, how you might use your mind to learn to perform more effectively is simply not on the agenda.

It is as if there is a conspiracy of silence when it comes to learning to learn. We invest huge sums of money in business processes, in research and development, in computer systems, and in management training, but almost nothing in understanding how the minds of our employees and colleagues work—or, indeed, how our own mind functions.

Nevertheless, talk to most managers today and it is the quality of their people that is apparently critical to their success. The old ingredients like price and product are taking second place to the way your people deal with your customers. This unique resource—people's ability to learn—is arguably the only source of competitive advantage naturally available to all organizations, and it is so often ignored.

There can be little doubt that how we learn is central to success in today's fast-changing world. As the great educator John Holt put it in the 1960s:

Since we cannot know what knowledge will be most needed in the future, it is senseless to try and teach it in advance. Instead we should try to turn out people who love learning so much and learn so well that they will be able to learn whatever needs to be learned.

This is as true today as it was 40 years ago. But our understanding of how our brains work has advanced along with the extraordinary speed of technical change, so that common sense and science may well have caught up with each other at last.

> **What have you ever been taught or learned about how you learn to learn? Ask your friends and family. What do you know about how your mind works?**

By reading this book and taking time to reflect on the knowledge that is lying hidden beneath the surface of your life, you will be able to power up your own mind and the minds of those with whom you work and live.

TAKING YOUR MIND OUT OF ITS BOX

Imagine you have just bought a computer or some electrical item for the home. You are unpacking it for the first time. As you undo the brown cardboard box, you are faced with various bits and pieces, some wrapped in plastic, some further packed in polystyrene. You recognize some things, while others perplex you. For a few brief moments you have a glimpse of the workings of some mechanical object before it has become a familiar part of your life. At the bottom of the box is a manual telling you how to put the bits together, how to get started, and how to get the best out of the product you have bought.

Most people have this kind of experience several times a year. We find out the basics of how an item of equipment works. With a more complex item, say a camera, we may go on to learn new techniques to ensure that we can use it effectively. We may acquire various guides to help us to take better pictures. Most of us who drive a car occasionally have to read its manual before trying to fix an indicator light that is not working. From time to time, we may even peer at the engine, seeking to coax it into life, although we may know very little about how the car works. Certainly, we need to fill the car up with fuel and water on a regular basis.

Yet, when it comes to our mind most of us know less about it than we know about the engine of our car. Our mind is so much a part of us, from our first memories onward, that we never stop to admire it or wonder how it works.

This book is going to help you "unpack" your mind, so that you can "reassemble" the component elements. Then, as with a camera, you can begin to use this "manual" to help you find out what your mind needs to work more effectively, to power it up.

Imagine you are "unpacking" your mind for the first time. Let's start with your brain—although this is not all there is to your mind, as we will see later.

Imagine that you could take off the hard outside covering of the skull and look at what you have. It is a grey, slimy, slightly wobbly mass of human tissue. If you were able to bring yourself to hold it in your hands, it would weigh a little more than a typical bag of sugar.

Without doubt, you would be looking at the most complex piece of machinery in the world. It has been compared to a hydraulic system, a loom, a telephone exchange, a theater, a sponge, a city, and, not surprisingly, a computer. But it is more complicated than any of these. And, although we are still comparatively ignorant, we have begun to find out a little more about how it works in the last few decades.

In the next few pages you will find out some of the basic science underpinning the operation of your mind.

However, let me start with a health warning. As with all simple explanations of deeply complex issues, there is a danger that too much can be read into a few short paragraphs. Inevitably, this leads to disappointment. On the other hand, if you see what follows as a number of different ways of looking at your mysterious mind, possibly as metaphors, then you may find that more helpful. The neuroscientist Professor Susan Greenfield put it like this at a Royal Institution seminar:

It does not matter that popular science may not get things completely right; at least it offers a mental model for what is going on inside the brain.

YOUR THREE BRAINS

In 1978 Paul Maclean proposed the idea that we have three brains, not one. This is a difficult notion to grasp, but stay with it for a moment. Imagine you can reach forward and remove the two outer brains: they will come away quite easily and you will be left with an apricot-sized object (see Figure 1). This is sometimes called your primitive or reptilian brain; as its name suggests, it is the bit that

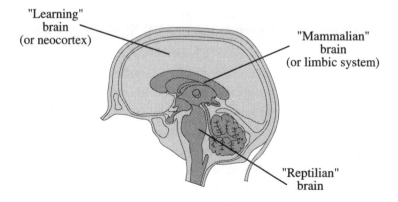

Figure 1 Three brains

even simple creatures like reptiles have. It governs your most basic survival instincts, for example whether, if threatened, you will stay to fight or run away. It seems also to control other basic functions such as the circulation of your blood, your breathing, and your digestion.

Now retrieve the smaller of the two "brains" that you took off earlier. It is shaped a bit like a collar and fits around the reptilian brain. It is sometimes referred to as your limbic system, after the Latin word *limbus* meaning border. This is the part of your brain that you share with most mammals. Scientists think it deals with some of the important functions driving mammals, for example, processing emotions, dealing with the input of the senses and with long-term memories.

Finally, pick up the outer, third brain. This is the part that sits behind your forehead and wraps around the whole of your mammalian brain. (Think of one of your hands held horizontally and palm downward, gripping your other hand that you have clenched into a fist.) You probably recognize this bit! It is the stuff of science fiction movies to see its crinkled and lined shape swimming in a glass jar of liquid. It is the most advanced of your three brains, your learning brain. It deals with most of the higher-order thinking and functions.

In evolutionary terms, your small, reptilian brain is the oldest and the outer, learning brain is the most recently acquired. Thinking about the brain in this way helps us see how human beings have progressed from primitive life forms. It also helps to explain in a very simple way why we cannot learn when we are under severe stress. In such situations it is as if a magic lever is pulled telling our outer learning brain to turn off and retreat, for survival's sake, to our primitive brain. Here the choice is quite simple, flight or fight. It leaves no room for subtlety of higher thinking. At various stages throughout this book you will be able to find out how to avoid creating just such an unhelpful response.

Scientists are increasingly sure, however, that Maclean's theories, sometimes known as the idea of the triune brain, are an oversimplification of the way the brain works. In fact, it is much more "plastic" and fluid in how it deals with different functions. Many parts of the brain can learn to perform new functions and there is much unused capacity.

YOUR DIVIDED BRAIN

Put the three parts of your brain back together and pause to admire them! Imagine you are a magician doing a trick with an orange, which you have secretly cut in half beforehand. You tap the orange and it magically falls neatly into two halves, a right and a left hemisphere, before an astonished audience. Imagine your brain falling into two halves, with the same startling effect.

The ancient Egyptians first noticed that the left side of our brain appeared to control the right half of our body, and vice versa. More recently and more significantly, in the 1960s Roger Sperry discovered that the two halves of the brain are associated with very different activities. It was he who first cut through the connection between them, known as the corpus callosum.

For many centuries before this, scientists thought that we had two brains, just as we have two kidneys, two ears, and two eyes. Work on stroke patients, however, where parts of their brains have been damaged, gives us some interesting further clues. It seems that the left side mainly handles sequential, mathematical, and logical issues, while the right is more creative and associative in the way it works. The left is literal, while the right enjoys metaphorical interpretation. The two sides perform different functions, the left side, for example, dealing with much of the brain's language work.

Roger Ornstein, in *The Right Mind*, has since gone further in showing how the two halves actually work together and how the right side has a special role in dealing with the more complex overall meaning of many of the issues we face today.

Indeed, the idea of being left- or right-brained is becoming more commonly used in business. Ned Hermann, while working at General Electric, translated much of this into useful insights for the workplace, exploring how each of us has inbuilt preferences toward the left or the right side of our brains. The left brain is the more logical and rational half. It makes judgments and relies on the intellect. It likes to do things one at a time and plays by the rules. The right side is the source of our intuition and imagination. It is playful and likes to take great leaps of thought. It enjoys creating new patterns and solutions.

Hermann takes the idea that our brains have two halves and adds to it a theory that we have already met, that higher-order thinking takes place at the top of your "learning" brain, while the more basic emotional functions are located at the bottom, toward the "reptilian" brain.

Hermann suggests that your instinctive characteristics will be different depending on which side and which "quarter" of your brain is dominant. Your brain is, in a sense, hot-wired to lead you to want to act in certain ways.

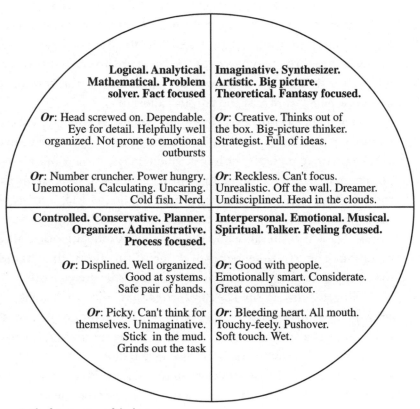

Logical. Analytical. Mathematical. Problem solver. Fact focused

Or: Head screwed on. Dependable. Eye for detail. Helpfully well organized. Not prone to emotional outbursts

Or: Number cruncher. Power hungry. Unemotional. Calculating. Uncaring. Cold fish. Nerd.

Imaginative. Synthesizer. Artistic. Big picture. Theoretical. Fantasy focused.

Or: Creative. Thinks out of the box. Big-picture thinker. Strategist. Full of ideas.

Or: Reckless. Can't focus. Unrealistic. Off the wall. Dreamer. Undisciplined. Head in the clouds.

Controlled. Conservative. Planner. Organizer. Administrative. Process focused.

Or: Displined. Well organized. Good at systems. Safe pair of hands.

Or: Picky. Can't think for themselves. Unimaginative. Stick in the mud. Grinds out the task

Interpersonal. Emotional. Musical. Spiritual. Talker. Feeling focused.

Or: Good with people. Emotionally smart. Considerate. Great communicator.

Or: Bleeding heart. All mouth. Touchy-feely. Pushover. Soft touch. Wet.

Figure 2 The four quarters of the brain

I have deliberately used two kinds of language in Figure 2. The first set of words is neutral, while the second and third are more obviously biased, the kind of things you might hear in an office or from teenagers at home!

Throughout *Power Up Your Mind*, you will be finding out

about ways of analyzing yourself as a learner. It is very important to realize that there are no right or wrong ways of approaching life and learning. Each is equally valuable. Each characteristic is capable of being described positively and negatively. And the most important thing of all is that you can change the way you do things. You can learn to work and live smarter!

In many workplaces, left-brain characteristics appear to be the ones that are most valued. Increasingly, however, the more creative elements offered by right-brain thinking are being acknowledged as just as important.

If you have developed the capacity to use your brain effectively, then you will be able to use positive words from all of the segments to describe your behavior at work. In other words, you will have learned how to acquire a range of different characteristics.

Where would you put yourself? Do you have more right- or left-brained characteristics? Which words match your characteristics most? What about those with whom you work closely? What mix of left- and right-brain characteristics do you think you need to have in a successful team?

Dividing our brains up into imaginary quarters in this way is another huge oversimplification, although it is biologically true that we do have two hemispheres in our brain connected by the corpus callosum. We now know, for example, through the work of Stanislaus Dehaen, that a simple mathematical sum, which you might assume was a left-brain function, is much more complex. If you express a problem as "What is two plus two?" you are probably using the left hemisphere. But if you reframe the question as "$2 + 2 = ?$" it is likely that you will use brain areas in both the right and left sides.

In fact, as Roger Ornstein and others have pointed out, there is almost nothing that we do that is governed by only one side. Moreover, we have found out that stroke victims can learn to use their undamaged side for tasks previously undertaken by the other side.

Nevertheless, it is interesting to think of the different approaches that seem to be dominant in the two different halves of the brain. With a mental model like this we can begin to explore apparently conflicting approaches to life, the dynamic tensions between the logical and the intuitive. Of course, it is never a simple question of "either/or," just as neuroscience shows that it is rarely a simple issue of "right" or "left."

As with the idea that we have three brains not one, thinking about your brain's two halves gives you a visual model to help you begin to understand why certain people behave in different ways.

And just as our extraordinary brain demonstrates its plasticity and flexibility, so we can learn to adapt and change our behavior beyond the quarter that may instinctively dominate for each of us.

CLOSE-UP ON YOUR BRAIN

The greatest unexplored territory in the world is the space between our ears.
William O'Brien, former President of Hanover Insurance

Now return to the task of unpacking your mind. Put the two halves together again and zoom in on your brain with an imaginary microscope. The grey jelly-like matter that you can see is, on closer inspection, made up of brain cells, some 100 billion of them. Understanding how these cells work offers some important clues about the way we learn and work.

Discovered by Camillo Golgi and Santiago Ramon y Cajal a century ago, the cells are also called neurons. Each has the potential to connect with another, reaching out a "tentacle" called an axon. Each neuron has other tentacles called dendrites that it uses to receive incoming signals from another neuron's axon (see Figure 3). The minute gap between axons is called a synapse.

It is at this detailed level that the brain is operating when you learn, have a thought, remember something, feel aroused, or undertake any of the other myriad functions dealt with by your brain. One cell connects chemically and electrically with another and a neural pathway or synaptic connection is made. Your dendrites "learn" from other cells by receiving messages and the cell, in turn, "teaches" other cells by passing on information through its axon. It is the number of connections, not the number of cells, that is important. Just as any electrical appliance has wires bringing the current in and wires

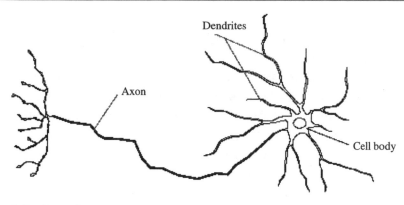

Figure 3 Dendrites and axons

going out to complete the circuit, so your nerve cells are connected. And you don't need to be a rocket scientist to see that there are plenty of potential connections to be made in any one brain.

We learn by experience, by interacting with the world using our senses. Connections or pathways develop between neurons, which become the routes through which we access our experiences. When we think or learn, the neural networking that is taking place is, at a microchemical level, our brain learning from our experiences.

When stimulated, neurons grow many dendrites. These look like twigs from a branch and connect with an axon from another neuron or group of neurons. In fact, the dendrites and axons can connect with each other at various points along their length. When they connect, they are literally exchanging a small electrical charge and also releasing minute amounts of different chemicals, depending on the nature of the experience.

The first time we learn something we are comparatively slow. I picture my dendrites as explorers, beating a path through a jungle. The next time it is easier because there is already a route cut out. Scientists think that this may involve a substance called myelin, which coats and insulates axons, ensuring much faster transmission of impulses. Scientists also tell us that water is essential for the effective movement of the dendrites in your brain, just as it is for the passage of any explorer through unexplored terrain.

We have three different kinds of neuron. One group brings information from our senses, another has a networking role using their dendrites to connect to other neurons in our brain, and the third group conveys messages from our brain to our muscles and gets our bodies to act accordingly. We sense, we process, and then we act in some way, sometimes consciously, sometimes unconsciously. What we store in amazingly complex patterns of neural connections is the basis of our learning and our memory and, taken all together, is at the heart of our developing personality.

Put at its most simple, the more you learn, the more you are powering up your brain. You create more connections or synapses when you learn and it is the amount of synapses in your brain that determines your capacity, not the number of neurons or brain cells.

If you are interested in finding out more about the science of what is happening in your brain, books and television programs by Professor Susan Greenfield are an excellent place to start. She manages to convey what we know and what we are still finding out about how our brains work in language that is immediate and vivid.

A good way of being sure that you have understood something is to be able to teach someone else. See if you can tell someone at work or at home the basics of what is going on in your brain when you learn, using what you have read so far. You might like to see if you could draw a simple picture from memory of the workings of your brain.

FIVE KEY PRINCIPLES

Along with the other things that you have found out as you unpacked your brain, it is helpful to appreciate some of the principles that underlie the operating systems of your mind.

1   The brain loves to explore and make sense of the world

You have seen how your axons and dendrites are constantly seeking to establish new networks, to process and store knowledge. Your brain is endlessly seeking to make sense of what it experiences. Your brain is continually searching for new data, for new experiences. Like your dendrites and axons, it is very determined.

An important consequence is that, to ensure that your brain is powered up, you nccd to give it as many new experiences as possible, as well as the time to make sense of them. Another practical result is that, like any explorer, your brain tends to do better when it has a map or at least knows where it is going!

2   The brain likes to make connections

As you have seen, the way that the brain learns is by making connections. Axons and dendrites link together to enable meaning and learning to flow from one neuron to another.

In fact, your brain is so good at making connections that it will often try to fill in the gaps even when it is missing information. You see a cat moving along behind a fence and, although part of the cat's body is obscured by the posts of the fence, your brain fills in the rest and thinks it is seeing a complete cat. Or when someone tells us a half-truth or only gives us part of the information we need, our brain immediately starts to make up the missing bits. If you are trying to solve a problem, this tendency is a positive one. But if you are trying to communicate to your colleagues or family and only give part of the story, it can lead to suspicion, gossip, and unease for other people as their brains try to fill in the gaps.

3   The brain thrives on patterns

As your neurons establish the same or similar connections with each other over time, so patterns are established. Pattern making is at the heart of your brain's filing system, its ability to make sense of what it has learned. If you have never seen a lion, the first time one rushes at you you may think it is some kind of horse. Assuming you survive this ordeal, the next time one attacks you will make yourself scarce. Your brain has noticed that a creature with a tawny mane and a worrying roar is not going to be friendly. A pattern has been established. All lions appearing in the future will be "filed" in the part of the brain labeled "dangerous animals."

Our ability to make patterns is at the heart of our civilization. We organize our communities into houses and streets and towns. We lay out road networks. We create languages and number systems. Interestingly, this very positive attribute can also limit our potential when certain patterns become ingrained and we consequently become resistant to change.

4   The brain loves to imitate

Allied to pattern making is the brain's capacity for imitation. Until a synaptic connection has been made there is no "knowledge," except what we are born with. The most efficient way for connections to be established is by watching what others do and copying them. So, we learn to speak and talk when we are young by watching and listening to others. We learn many social customs by observation.

The capacity of the brain to mimic others is important. "Sitting next to Nellie," as it is sometimes called, is a great way to learn. The use of role models and modeling certain behaviors at home and at work are powerful methods of passing on learning. In the workplace, coaches help to accelerate this process of intelligent imitation. In most families, much of the learning takes the form of copying other family members.

5   The brain does not perform well under too much stress

Your brain has evolved from the bottom upward. The most primitive functions are at the bottom of your brain, the brain stem. It is here that rapid decisions of life and death are taken, those normally referred to as "fight or flight." If your reptilian brain and cerebellum perceive a major threat to your survival, they have to act fast. In practice, they trigger the release of chemicals like adrenaline and noradrenaline (also known as epinephrine and norepinephrine), which put your body into a state of heightened arousal. Either your arms and legs begin to fight your attacker or your legs start to move rapidly as you flee from the scene.

When your brain is under severe stress, it can only think of survival. Blood and energy that would otherwise be available for higher-order thinking in your mammalian and learning brains are simply diverted into ensuring that you live to fight another day.

This is not the same thing as saying that all stress is bad for you. On the contrary, without the challenge on which your brain also thrives, you simply would not grow and evolve. Nevertheless, few people find it easy to think about complex issues when they are staring disaster in the face. For effective learning to take place there needs to be a balance between high challenge and low threat.

Think back over the last 24 hours. What have you consciously explored? What new connections or conclusions have you made? How have you categorized the things that have happened to you recently? What have you admired and who was doing it? Might you imitate them? Think of all the ways in which you make sense of the world around you, the links you make in your everyday life, the way you process and "file" experiences, and the capacity you have for learning by copying others. Have you been under undue stress recently? Or was the balance of threat and challenge such that you enjoyed the experience?

BRAIN OR MIND?

So far so good with respect to the brain. But is brain the same as mind?

There has long been uncertainty about this. In the seventeenth century, René Descartes argued that the mind and body were completely separate, joining in the pineal gland. Against the background of this kind of dogmatic view, it was hardly surprising that, in the nineteenth century, Thomas Hewitt Key was able to puzzle: "What is mind? No matter. What is matter? No mind."

Most people would agree that, while brain and mind are often used interchangeably, they do not mean exactly the same. Isolated from its body, a brain is just that, not a mind. Yet, if we are asked where our mind is, most of us point to our head. Does mind describe the larger functions, while brain tends to be used to describe the neural circuitry? Are our emotions and values part of our mind? Where do our values and beliefs come in?

This sort of question does not have any simple answers. But it seems clear that "mind" is somehow a more inclusive term than "brain." For me, the simplest way of describing a mind is:

Brain + Personality = Mind

In this book we will be applying what we know about the brain, about emotions, about values, and about key elements of personality. I will use both brain and mind throughout the book, just as most of us would in our everyday conversations.

BRAIN FOOD

If this were a user's guide to a piece of electrical equipment like a computer, then early on there would be some advice on setting it up and looking after it. So, what about the brain? How you should you feed and care for it?

There are two kinds of revolution taking place on today's High Street. The first is the explosion of health and fitness centers and gyms, the growth of healthy, often organic food, and the carrying of water bottles as a lifestyle item. The second is the burgeoning empire of coffee shops and the ever-increasing amount of packaged food with high levels of sugar and salt. While the first of these is obviously positive for your brain, the second can be unhelpful.

You may be wondering if there is a magic, brain-friendly meal or diet that will enhance the way you use your brain. Sadly this is not the case, although there are some useful principles that you can apply. When Virginia Woolf wrote, "One cannot think well, love well, sleep well if one has not dined well," she was only roughly right, depending on what and when she was eating! Your mind, like the rest of your body, thrives on a balanced diet.

The three key principles with regard to food are:

1   Hydration
2   Balance
3   Little and often.

The first principle is that your brain needs to be fully hydrated to function effectively. You need to drink several liters of water a day for your brain's "circuitry" to work well, more if you are also eating food that is diuretic. Many people are, in fact, permanently living in a state of partial dehydration in which their brains work considerably below their capacity. It is difficult to power up your mind if its circuitry lacks the water it needs to function effectively. A study by Trevor Brocklebank at Leeds University in the UK found that schoolchildren with the best results in class were those who drank up to eight glasses of water a day.

When I was interviewing business leaders for this book, I asked them various questions about how they look after their brains. Jayne-Anne Gadhia, managing director of Virgin One Account, has noticed improvements in performance since she and her senior team started drinking more water.

Secondly, you need a balanced diet. Not surprisingly, different foods have different effects. Proteins such as egg, yoghurt, fish, chicken, and pork contain the amino acid tyrosine. This is broken down to create two useful chemicals called neurotransmitters, norephrine and dopamine, which both promote alertness and the effective functioning of memory. More complex carbohydrates such as vegetables, rice, and fruit create the amino acid tryptophan, which slows the brain down.

Fats produce acetylchline, which, in reasonable amounts, is good for your memory and for the overall health of your neural networks. We tend to eat too much fat. We also eat too much sugary food. Simple carbohydrates such as sugars give you a quick burst of energy, although, as those who take care how they combine their foods will know, it depends what you have with them as to exactly how they affect you. A popular form of sugar is chocolate. This also contains the chemical theobromine, which causes short-term arousal, possibly why it is commonly enjoyed after a late meal!

Salts are essential to the healthy functioning of all cells. Specifically, there needs to be a balance between sodium and potassium salts. However, most people eat too much sodium, typically in crisps and processed foods. Salty food, in its turn, produces the need to drink more water.

Caffeine, taken from coffee or tea, is widely enjoyed the world over. It is a stimulant, producing an effect not unlike the release of cortisol when your adrenal gland is working strongly. The brain becomes alert over a short period, explaining why coffee helps to keep you awake at night. Too much coffee, however, causes dizziness, headaches, and difficulty in concentrating. Coffee is also a diuretic, so for every cup you drink you need at least two of water.

Alcohol is widely enjoyed and, in reasonable amounts, is a useful element of a balanced diet. It causes a loss of inhibitions and so, for some, enhances confidence and helps them to be more creative. Alcohol is also a depressant and too much of it reduces the flow of blood to the front cortex area of your brain, so making you less effective as a thinker. In addition, it is a diuretic, as anyone who has drunk too much knows to their cost when they wake up the next morning.

Various additives commonly found in processed food affect the brain adversely. This is most pronounced when you are young: for example, there is ample research to connect additives with unhelpful levels of hyperactivity in school pupils, at an age when their brains are much more demanding of energy and must have good food and drink to create this.

We need a balanced diet of all the ingredients above. For many of us this means eating less fat, less salt, and less chocolate, and drinking less coffee, less tea, and less alcohol. For some of us it may mean reviewing the amount of protein we eat. And for most of us it means eating more fresh fruit and vegetables.

The third principle is to eat little and often, what is sometimes describes as a "grazing" diet.

After a big meal, your stomach and digestive system are hungrily consuming oxygenated blood. This is why you tend to feel sleepy after a big meal: your brain is literally being denied enough blood to function at a high level of alertness. Although grazing has unfortunate associations with snacking on chocolate and potato chips, if the basic ingredients are good it ensures consistent levels of energy through the day.

What is your own diet like? Are you conscious of the cause and effect of what you eat and how your mind works? Do you sag after lunch? Could you change your diet to help you perform more consistently at any time of day?

Most people find it helpful to have a good breakfast after not having eaten for many hours. And even if you do not feel hungry, you may well find it beneficial to eat a fruit such as a banana before you go to work.

LAUGHTER, MUSIC, AND SLEEP

There are other ways of feeding the mind. When the eighteenth-century writer Joseph Addison said that "man is distinguished from all other creatures by the faculty of laughter," he was not only correct but also, perhaps unwittingly, drawing attention to a vital characteristic of our species. Did you know that children laugh some 300 times a day, whereas we miserable adults are closer to 50 if we're lucky?

Laughter is important because when we laugh we reduce our stress levels. Laughter leads to a decrease in the amount of cortisol flowing through our system. That is why it is always helpful when someone diffuses a difficult situation by making us laugh. Research has shown that laughter also improves the immune system and leads to better problem solving.

What do you do to make sure there is enough laughter in your life?

Music is another source of comfort. There are quite a few misleading claims currently being made for the effect of music on the brain, mainly by those with a proprietary product to sell to parents wanting the best for their growing child! Unfortunately, just as there is no magic formula for a brain-expanding diet, you cannot become more naturally intelligent simply by listening to certain kinds of music. Nor will listening to music guarantee a good memory.

However, research has shown that music, as well as being extremely enjoyable, can help in a number of ways. It seems that when we listen to music, both sides of the brain are involved in processing the melodies and patterns. This would seem to suggest that listening to music engages a significant amount of our brain and that it may be good preparation for learning.

Certainly, we know that music can reduce stress levels, aid relaxation, and influence our mood. Our heart beat, for example, will reduce in speed if we are listening to music with a slow, stately beat. Repetitive music can help induce a state of trance. And the soothing undulation of a lullaby has for generations sent us to sleep as infants!

Georgi Lozanov suggests that different kinds of music affect us differently. Classical and romantic music is an ideal accompaniment to taking in new information, while baroque is better for processing or reviewing information. Many people find that music inspires them to be more creative.

A growing number of people assert that they remember things better to music, but I have not yet seen any conclusive evidence and prefer to remain open-mindedly agnostic about it. Common sense would suggest that, in some situations, music will be competing for the learner's attention, while in others it may helpfully complement it. It would also seem to be the case that different personalities respond differently to music.

What do you think? How do you like to use music in your life? Do you use it in your learning? If so, what kinds of activities are particularly enhanced by the addition of music?

Sleep is another way of feeding our mind. What is most important about sleep is that our brain needs more of it than we currently tend to have. Although individual needs differ, and generally as we get older we need less sleep, most of us function best on about seven and a half hours. There are well-known exceptions, of course, like Margaret Thatcher, who apparently only needed a few hours.

However, for most people, if we don't get enough sleep, then, not surprisingly, our brain functions at well below its capacity. That is why sleep deprivation is an effective way of breaking down people's resistance.

Sir Michael Bichard, Permanent Secretary at the Department for Education and Employment in the UK, was categorical in his thinking about this: "I know I am much more effective when I am fresher and fitter." And yet, in some circles, it is almost a badge of honor to talk of late nights and excessive hours working, as if they merited congratulation rather than sympathetic disapproval!

It is not simply the number of hours' sleep that matters. During the day, your mind is constantly taking in new experiences. Our brain needs deep sleep, sometimes called REM sleep (rapid eye movement), when we are also often dreaming. It is at these times that your brain is processing the experiences of the day.

Studies in animals have shown that the neurotransmitter acetylcholine is being produced in REM sleep, a chemical essential for healthy neural networks and therefore for memory. Consequently, deep sleep has been shown to aid the process of forming memories. When your brain is asleep, its speed slows right down for most of the time, producing what are called theta and delta waves. Recently it has been suggested that, during REM sleep, your brain also transmits at an extremely fast rate, about 40 cycles per second, and these have been called gamma waves.

It is no accident that you say you will "sleep on it." A number of researchers have noticed that if you review something before you go to sleep and again when you wake up, you tend to remember more of it. I know this works for me. When I have a particularly complex presentation to make, I find this technique helps me to master my subject much more effectively.

Jayne-Anne Gadhia consciously uses the power of sleep:

I go to bed worrying about something and when I wake up I have an answer. I now deliberately pop a question into my mind before I go to sleep and ask myself the answer in the morning as I take my shower!

In fact, when we are asleep, we go through a number of cycles, each taking about one and a half hours, each moving from a lighter sleep into a deeper sleep and back again. Going through a number of these complete cycles is critical for our mental health.

Darkness is important for encouraging the pineal gland to produce the neurotransmitter melatonin, an essential chemical for ensuring that our body clock functions effectively. A dramatic example of how our brains are affected by upset time rhythms is experienced whenever we fly across major time zones. (It turns out that our natural body clock is closer to the lunar cycle of 25 hours rather than the solar rhythm of 24 hours.)

It is has been confirmed that there really are some people who favor the mornings and some the evenings. There are also distinctly better times of the day for doing things. In the mornings, most people take in new information best, while the afternoons—except immediately after lunch—are better for reviewing and processing. However, there are significant individual variations from this general pattern.

Days are, broadly speaking, times for taking in experiences, nights for processing them. In addition, at a micro level within the day, Georgi Lozanov has suggested that we need to aim for periods of high energy, then relaxation, then energy, then relaxation, and so on.

Most of this is common sense. But somehow, perhaps because we lead such busy lives, the powerful role of sleep is often forgotten, as are the natural cycles that necessitate processing time as well as task time.

Think back over the last week. Have there been days when you have been conscious of under-performance due to lack of sleep? Do you try to build in relaxation moments as well as more energetic ones? Are you a morning or an evening person?

Of course, the stimulation afforded by other people and the excitement of new experiences are other major sources of nourishment, just as altogether quieter moments can be.

NEARLY UNPACKED

You have now nearly finished unpacking your brain—but do you really need to know any of this stuff? Does the chemistry of your mind have any bearing on your success as an individual? Would you work smarter if you knew a little more? Is all this just common sense anyway? Or would it be better to plug your mind in, start to use it, and leave the worrying about how it works to brain scientists?

By the time you have read this book, you will have seen many ways in which you can power up your mind and improve your performance. You should have learned more than 100 simple and realistic things that you can do to make you more successful by using your brain more effectively.

Before you move on, read the following story of a typical senior business executive called Annie. In it there are at least 20 examples of how your mind can be positively or negatively affected by how you treat it. I have picked out 10 examples and in the next chapter you can find some of the practical ways in which you can look after your mind more effectively. When you have finished reading Power Up Your Mind, *you should be able to add many others.*

A DAY IN THE LIFE OF ANNIE'S BRAIN

When Annie woke up she was already beginning to regret last night's party. After only five hours' sleep, her head hurt and her mouth felt dry. A full glass of water beside the bed reminded her that she had meant to drink it before her head hit the pillow.

She looked at her alarm clock with horror. Only an hour to go before her first meeting at 9 o'clock. And today was when she needed an important decision from her new boss, Stephen, one that had been preying on her mind for the last week. Two large cups of espresso coffee later and a quick shower, and she was out of the door and on her way to her office. Another typical day was beginning and her mind was already racing. Annie found herself idly wondering how it was that she never quite realized her potential at work, then dismissed the thought from her brain as she drove into the car park of Anydeal.com.

"So, let's get started," said John to Geoff and the others around the table. "I haven't done an agenda as we all know what needs to be sorted out. Let's just work our way through until we finish."

Three cups of coffee and two hours later, the meeting over, Annie got up from her chair and moved over to the window. It was funny how much better merely standing up made her feel. She looked at her scribbled notes of the meeting she had just had. She found herself realizing that she couldn't remember a single thing. She hadn't known what the meeting was going to be about and had, in truth, switched off after only 20 minutes of being talked at by Geoff as he went through an interminable PowerPoint™ presentation.

She decided to wander out to the water machine. Standing beside it, she drank glass after glass of water and then sped back to her office.

Apart from a mountain of paperwork and email, she had two main things she wanted to achieve that day: to hold the attention of her project team for a very important planning meeting, and to try to convince her boss, the new managing director, that she needed another three members of staff if they were to complete their work on time.

Back in the office, she got straight down to her administrative work, even though she still had a nagging headache. Apart from a few calls, she worked pretty much uninterrupted up to lunchtime. A quick stroll in the park, a large bottle of water and a sandwich later, and she was ready for her meeting.

As Annie's team came into her office, she made sure that she had a quick word with each of them, establishing their mood and trying to make them feel relaxed but alert. She spent several minutes with Paul who was presenting the main part of the session. He always pleasantly surprised her, and it looked like today was not going to be an exception.

Paul started by reminding the team why they were meeting and checking everyone's agreement over where they needed to get to by five o'clock. Paul had an amusing way with words and the ability to create mental pictures, which had all of the team laughing out loud as he described the situation they were in. Annie found herself relaxing and engaging in a way she had not done in her earlier meeting.

Then, instead of relying on a PowerPoint presentation, Paul asked the eight members of the team to pair up and spend a few minutes role-playing the job of explaining to the rest of their staff why the project was three months behind schedule. Each pair then gave a bravura snippet from their role-play to the whole group. There was a great deal of laughter and Annie made a mental note to use the idea herself, especially in a meeting after lunch when people's attention often seemed to drop.

Then Paul turned over a flipchart sheet he had prepared earlier. On it was a very clear mind map™ of the options they faced, expressed visually. Finally, he gave a short verbal account of his own view of the next steps and turned to Annie to chair the rest of the meeting.

"That was great, Paul. I specifically liked the way you got us on our feet at the beginning: it really seemed to engage all of our attention and I feel that we have all really bought into the problems that we face as a result."

The rest of the meeting was a delight. Building on the excellent start Paul had made, Annie started by breaking the challenges they faced down into small chunks that were accessible enough for them all to deal with. Every 20 or 30 minutes she gave everyone a quick stretch break, except once when they all agreed that they were flowing too well to break their concentration. They finished at 5, with a clear summary from her, confident that they had agreed a really good plan to manage their next few months' work.

After the meeting, Annie headed up the corridor to the office of her new boss, Stephen.

As she went in, Stephen was in deep conversation on the phone and motioned for her to sit down. Five minutes passed and Annie found herself wondering whether she had got the time of the meeting right. For a moment she almost felt afraid, with her mind frozen into unaccustomed incoherence. But before she could check her diary, Stephen slammed the phone down and looked expectantly at her.

Annie always found this habit of Stephen's disconcerting. Her heart beat faster and she could feel her well-rehearsed thoughts flying out of her head. In truth, there was something about Stephen that terrified her, reminding her of a much-hated headmaster she had once had.

"So, you want me to throw more money at this lousy project, do you?" This was more of a statement than a question.

"Well..." Annie began, but was cut off.

"Look, Annie, when I gave you this assignment, we both agreed it would be tough. I'm sorry, but there's no way I can support you on this. We're already way over budget. It just wouldn't give out the right messages. Look, I've got to see the kids tonight. Would you mind if we called it a day?"

With that, Stephen swept out, leaving Annie on her own.

All her positive feelings about her afternoon meeting evaporated in an instant. She felt miserable. Gathering up her papers, she headed back to her office and went home as soon as she could.

Still, at least she was going to see Peter for dinner tonight. He always listened to her stories and made her feel good about herself.

Maybe she might just have that early night she was always promising herself.

Annie doesn't look after her brain as well as she could, nor are the conditions at her workplace entirely conducive to its successful performance. As you read this book you will learn many practical ways in which you can take more care of your brain. Here are 10 to get you started.

10 tips for treating your brain right

1   *Keep well hydrated*. Your brain needs plenty of water for its "electronic circuitry" to function effectively.
2   *Take regular stretch breaks*. Your brain needs lots of oxygenated blood to work well. Just standing up releases an extra 20 percent.
3   *Always give the big picture first*. Your brain is constantly trying to make connections, so giving the big picture in advance allows it time to make sense of things and gather together all it knows about a particular subject, even for someone who loves to focus on the details.
4   *Avoid talking at people for long periods*. Your mind can only absorb a certain amount of new data and unless the speaker is very talented it will switch off after 20 minutes or so.
5   *Vary the ways you give out information*. Our minds are all different, some preferring visual, some auditory, and some the kinesthetic experience of getting up and "doing" something.
6   *Think about concentration spans*. While it is helpful to stay on task when you are flowing well, regular short breaks every 20 or 30 minutes often help the mind to remain engaged.
7   *Break big things down into accessible bits*. Your brain finds it easier to deal with big issues when they are broken down into smaller elements.
8   *Use humor*. There is evidence that when you laugh your brain releases chemicals called endorphins that act as relaxants.
9   *Don't create fear in others if you want them to perform well*. Under stress our brains think only of survival and higher-order thinking stops happening effectively.

10   *Make sure you get enough sleep.* While each person's sleep requirement is different, a good night's sleep for many people involves more than seven hours. When your brain is tired it does not perform well.

Think back over the past 24 hours. How well have you been treating your brain? How many of the 10 simple tips above have you made good use of? Is your life like Annie's in any way?

UNPACKING YOUR MIND——IN A NUTSHELL

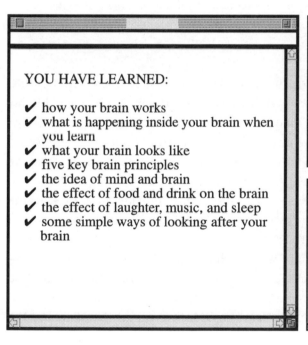

YOU HAVE LEARNED:

✔ how your brain works
✔ what is happening inside your brain when you learn
✔ what your brain looks like
✔ five key brain principles
✔ the idea of mind and brain
✔ the effect of food and drink on the brain
✔ the effect of laughter, music, and sleep
✔ some simple ways of looking after your brain

KEY IDEAS
The three brains
Left and right sides of the brain
Brain dominance
Neurons and synapses
Music and the mind
REM sleep

KEY TECHNIQUES/ APPROACHES
Drinking enough water
Eating a balanced diet
Having a laugh
Using music
Getting enough sleep

2

Getting Ready to Learn

If it be now, 'tis not to come; if it be not to come, it will be now; if it be not now, yet it will come: the readiness is all.

William Shakespeare, *Hamlet*

Hamlet spends much of Shakespeare's most famous play getting himself ready to deal with his suspicions of what has happened to his father. Many of us take a similar approach to learning.

When we are born we are clearly ready to learn. We have no preconceptions about ourselves. All our senses play on the amazing world we encounter. We watch, practice, and then walk. We listen, experiment, and then talk. Most homes provide an early learning environment that is good enough for us to walk, talk, and acquire a range of other useful skills.

As we grow up, we somehow become less ready. Other pressures bear down on us. We learn to worry and doubt. We can lose confidence. At home and at work, we can easily find our environment less conducive to learning than we would like it to be. We gather learning "baggage" around us, which begins to weigh us down.

But, unless we are ready to learn, we won't be able to realize our potential. When French scientist Louis Pasteur wrote that "chance favors only the prepared mind," he might have been talking about many "nonlearners" today, whose minds have become deprogrammed from the naturally receptive state in which they started life.

Have you ever stopped to wonder why when you go on a training course so little of it sticks? Or, if you have teenage children, why they often seem to be unready to learn? The chances are that you will probably have begun to appreciate that it is nearly all to do with your emotional or physical state. If you are tired or angry, hungry or distressed, too cold or too hot, you will not be in a state to learn. If you are being forced to do something when you are overwhelmed by some other issue, it can be hard to be ready to learn. If your body is out of condition, that also may have a bearing on your performance.

Being ready to learn is the part of the process of learning to learn that is most often overlooked. It is what Dr. Javier Bajer, chief executive of the Talent Foundation, calls being "primed" to learn. The analogy could not be clearer. When you are painting bare wood you need to smooth it and prepare it—prime it—before you start painting. If you don't, the paint won't stick properly. It is the same with learning: You need to be primed to learn or the learning won't stick. In fact, it will roll over you like water off a duck's back. This is why so much conventional training is a waste of money.

Recall the day in the life of Annie's brain and the way that Annie settled people at the start of the meeting. She was consciously trying to put them in the right emotional state from the beginning.

CHECKING YOUR EMOTIONAL READINESS

How emotionally ready are you to learn right now? How many of the following questions can you normally answer "no" to?

1 Are you feeling distressed?
2 Are you often too worried about your family to concentrate?
3 Are you often too worried about your work to concentrate?
4 Do you often feel bad about yourself?
5 Have you lost your sense of curiosity?
6 Are you normally too tired to concentrate?
7 Are you completely turned off learning and training?

If you answered "yes" to more than one of these questions, you may well have some work to do before you are ready to learn! Or it may be that the context in which you are answering these questions is not a good one for you today.

There are two aspects of being emotionally ready: the interior environment (what's going on inside your mind) and the exterior environment (what's going on outside, in the environment in which you find yourself). It is comparatively easy to change the latter, which is covered in the second half of Chapter 3, but more difficult to alter what is happening inside you.

As psychologist William James puts it:

The greatest revolution of our generation is the discovery that human beings, by changing the inner attitudes of their minds, can change the outer aspects of their lives.

CURIOSITY AND EMOTIONAL STATE

There are at least two elements to what may be going on inside your mind: your curiosity and your emotional state.

While we are all born curious, we seem to lose this instinct or at least dampen it down as we grow older. A young child will ask hundreds of questions in a typical day, but an adult asks only a few. Partly this is because children have a lot to find out and their curiosity is consequently very high. Partly, I am afraid to say, it is a result of the tendency of schools and other formal educational institutions to discourage the inquiring mind in its attempt to gather and assess knowledge. As American scientist Paul Maclean puts it:

It surprises me how our culture can destroy curiosity in the most curious of all animals—human beings.

Essentially, curiosity is a natural love of learning. It is the driver for much of the informal learning that we undertake. We want to find out how to grow a certain plant, how to cook a new meal, or where a particular word comes from. We are intrigued and it spurs us on to do something about it.

Some people seem to be more curious than others. Perhaps

their practical intelligence is very strong and they just have to find out how things work. However, you don't need to go much below the surface of most people to find something that interests them. That's why TV game shows, Trivial Pursuit, crosswords, and quizzes are popular with many adults.

In the UK, Ford has created one of the best-known employee development schemes, known as Ford EDAP. Under this scheme, each employee is given an amount of money and encouraged to go off and learn something that has no relationship to their job, but that stimulates their curiosity. These employees have found that you can relearn curiosity and get into the habit of enjoying asking questions. You can "reprogram" your brain to be curious.

What is your own curiosity rating? If you feel that you have lost your natural interest in finding out about the world around you, try these simple activities. What kinds of things do you like doing most at home? Make a list of your top five. Now make a similar list based on your work. Study your two lists. Are these things really of interest to you? Do they make you want to find out more?

Who do you admire most in the world? What do you think they are most interested in? If you have children, what area of their interest most appeals to you? See if you can focus on just one new area of interest and rekindle your curiosity in it.

If this doesn't work, try watching less television (unless you are deliberately using it as a source of information). Set aside one night a week to do something for yourself. You could try a new sport, learn to cook something, go for a walk somewhere you don't know, or search the web for new places to go on vacation.

Think of the person in your immediate circle at work, or someone important among your friends at home, who seems to be the most curious and interested in life, and spend some time with them. Listen for how they ask questions and how they show their appreciation when they find out something new. Try to imitate them, using your own style of language and approach. Ask them why they are curious about some things and not others.

For many people, not being emotionally ready to learn is the root cause of their inability to do so. One of the most common causes of this is fear.

Often, this comes about as the result of past experiences. The British Campaign for Learning carried out some telling research with a number of older men and women to find out their attitudes to learning. One 68-year-old man started crying when he recalled his experience of a particular lesson at school. The fear of his failure came rushing back to him, still powerful nearly six decades later.

Or it could be fear of a current threat. You have already discovered how the most primitive "fight or flight" mechanism is controlled by the most basic part of your brain. In crude evolutionary terms, it does not do for human beings to be musing on the meaning of life if there is a woolly mammoth bearing down on them at speed.

In too many workplaces today there are the contemporary equivalents of the woolly mammoth, who create a climate of threat around them. Not surprisingly, people in these situations find it difficult even to begin to think about learning.

In the 1970s, researchers showed that when we think we are under threat, we cease to perform effectively. We stop being able to pick up subtle clues, process information less well, become more limited in our range of behaviors, and tend to overreact.

Another common inhibiting factor is stress. We know that stress affects the brain's ability to function properly. US politician Dan Quayle famously misspelled potato by adding an extra "e" and a UK education minister failed to answer a simple multiplication sum correctly (7×8) under the stress of a BBC radio interview.

When we talk of something "completely going out of my head," we are referring to the fact that our minds don't function well under great stress. Many of us have memories of examination situations when we know we didn't perform to the best of our ability because of stress. Something similar is going on when actors dry up on stage.

A HIERARCHY OF EMOTIONAL NEEDS

The most famous description of this aspect of learning theory dates back to the 1940s and the work of psychologist Abraham Maslow. It grew out of his more general work to understand human motivation and is often referred to as a hierarchy of needs, running from physiological needs such as food and sleep, through safety, love, and belonging and esteem needs, to self-actualization needs, realizing your full potential.

Put simply, this means that you are unlikely to be able to switch yourself on to learn something if your most basic needs—having enough food, not being too tired, having a reasonable roof over your head, being safe, feeling loved, and feeling that you belong—are not met.

At first thought, getting to the top of this hierarchy seems suspiciously as if it might depend on material wealth. True, you need enough money to eat and to have somewhere to live. But money cannot buy love and belonging. And, most importantly, it cannot buy self-esteem.

> *What is your most powerful learning experience to date? What is the most stressful experience you can think of? What effect did it have on you? How did you get on at school? Do you experience threatening situations at work, causing you unacceptable stress? If so, what action could you take to improve this? Can you think of times when you have been on a training course and you felt too stressed to take in what you were learning? What could you have done to overcome this? Do you treat all of your colleagues with respect, even those you find most difficult to work with?*

READING YOUR OWN MOODS

Thinking about stress in the abstract is a difficult thing to do. It is much easier to describe your own mood at any one specific moment.

> *Try this activity right now. What kind of mood are you in? Use the mood meter overleaf to gauge how you are feeling.*
>
> *If you are running a meeting or seminar, it may be helpful to find out where your participants would position themselves on this meter. If they are down toward the bottom, then you will need to have strategies for dealing with them! They will not learn or participate effectively until they have started to deal with their negative feelings. More importantly, you will find it helpful to be more aware of your own moods as a learner.*

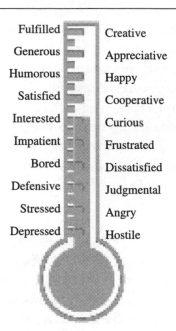

Fulfilled	Creative
Generous	Appreciative
Humorous	Happy
Satisfied	Cooperative
Interested	Curious
Impatient	Frustrated
Bored	Dissatisfied
Defensive	Judgmental
Stressed	Angry
Depressed	Hostile

AN EMOTIONALLY CONFUSING WORLD

Ever since Daniel Goleman's book, *Emotional Intelligence: Why it Can Matter More Than IQ*, there has been increasing acceptance of the role of emotions in the workplace. EQ has become a shorthand term for this aspect of intelligence and many very interesting tools and techniques have been developed as a result. But, in many cases, it is still talked about as if it were something distinctly separate from the rest of working life.

In truth, when it comes to dealing with emotions in the workplace we are still very much at first base. This is hardly surprising given the enormous variety of responses that the same event can produce in different people.

Take the case of Princess Diana. When she died in a car accident in Paris a few years ago, there were some interesting reactions. Prime Minister Tony Blair gave a long and moving speech in a churchyard suggesting that she was the princess of all our hearts. The leader of the British Opposition, William Hague, gave a rather short and uninvolved tribute. Ordinary people from all over the world sent flowers to Kensington Palace. Hundreds of thousands of these same ordinary people traveled to London to leave flowers as a mark of respect. The world's press camped out in London and Paris. The singer Elton John recorded a special version of "Candles in the Wind." A trust fund began to sell memorabilia—plates, mugs, pens—as if Diana were a saint. These ordinary items were sought by many as if they were holy relics. In contrast, many other people, both in private and in some serious articles in the press, attacked this national outpouring as being made up of bogus emotion for an ordinary but beautiful and rich media idol.

Who was right? What was an appropriate emotional response and what was not? Or were they all appropriate? The answers to these questions point up the difficulty of being sure any more, in these media-conscious days, of how to respond to something as universal as a tragic death.

Not surprisingly, it is equally difficult to establish exactly what place emotions should have in a contemporary workplace.

There were varying opinions from those I consulted. Jayne-Anne Gadhia thinks:

It is essential to show emotions, but in a controlled way. You must show passion and belief, but rarely anger. A leader needs to be able to touch people at a raw emotional level.

This last sentiment was echoed by many. Colin Marshall, chairman of British Airways, said:

It is a good thing for a leader to be seen as human. But one of a leader's most important responsibilities is keeping up employee morale and there will be times when uncertainty must be masked by a spirit of bravery. But you must always be truthful and realistic about prospects ahead.

Michael Bichard concurs with this need to motivate people by being real:

People relate to you as a human being. You do need to show emotion, but never fake it. Of course you have to display anger for effect sometimes.

Hilary Cropper, chief executive of the FI Group, inclines more toward the management of emotions:

I don't think you should show emotions at work. Yet you must obviously be emotional to make effective relationships. You have therefore, as a leader, to create a synthetic emotion, but one that is based on your genuine beliefs. Leadership is about deliberately creating a personality that is the right one for your company, and as such must involve playing a role. You need to be an actor, but it's not an act.

Joyce Taylor, managing director of Discovery Networks Europe, is more upbeat: "It is the positive emotions that are really important, elation, joy and optimism."

By contrast, the experienced industrial leader Sir Bob Reid, who has had to deliver some difficult news in his time, says:

It's very important to show you are really upset by some of the situations I've had to deal with in the oil and rail industries. Normally you must behave with equanimity, but for real issues, for example involving death, you must sometimes show your real emotions.

There would seem to be some negative emotions which are, by and large, unhelpful. These would include anger, fear, distress, and envy. By the same token, it would seem to be advantageous to show joy and pleasure.

But where does this list begin and end? What is appropriate and what is not? What do you think?

My one note of certainty is that we should all use what Stephen Covey calls the "pause button" a little more often. This is the internal switch we all have like the one on our video recorders. It puts us into a freeze-frame mode and gives us a few moments to calm down and reflect before going on with the action.

If you want people to feel wanted, then one of the most important things that any leader or manager in any organization needs to have in their emotional toolkit is the ability to show their appreciation of their staff appropriately. "I really appreciated the way you did that." "Thank you so much for staying on to help." "Thanks a lot, that made a real difference." These are just the beginnings of an important emotional lexicon that we all need to carry around with us and know how to use. For, as Antoine de Saint-Exupéry wrote in *The Little Prince*, "It is with the heart that one sees rightly; what is essential is invisible to the eye."

Even though we don't know how to deal with emotions, they certainly do have to be dealt with effectively, both at work and at home. One way of staying close to your own feelings is to keep a feelings file from time to time.

Try this idea. Take a page from your diary or personal organizer or create an electronic equivalent. Mark it out in hours and draw a line down the middle of the page. Every hour, stop and jot down on the left-hand side who you are with, where you are, and what you are doing. Describe on the right-hand side how you are feeling and any observations you might have about the situation. You can also use this approach in meetings if your attention is wandering!

RAISING SELF-ESTEEM

In an emotionally confusing world, maintaining your self-esteem is sometimes a hard task. Indeed, the concept of self-esteem needs some further explanation, for it is at the root of why so many people feel that they are not ready to learn. It is a hugely complex area with which, as a global society, we are only just beginning to get to grips. Self-esteem—how much you value yourself—is slippery stuff. One day you feel great. Then you lose your job or something devastating happens in your personal life and your esteem suddenly plummets.

Of course, loss of self-esteem can be much more subtle than this. Not doing as well as you would like to, feeling undervalued, feeling uncertain of your role: these are just some of the more common experiences leading to a lowering of self-esteem. Or it could be a single aspect of life that is going wrong and infecting all the rest, like a rotten apple in a fruit bowl.

Although it is always a good thing to give people positive feedback and seek to bolster their self-worth, if someone feels they are a failure, it may not help to tell them that in your eyes they are a success, because repeated failure is a sure way of lowering self-esteem.

Telling someone who has low self-esteem to cheer up or be more confident or pull themselves together is very unlikely to help. What they need to do is reprogram their mind and come up with new mental models to see them through the difficult time.

Martin Seligman has argued that it is important not to confuse low self-esteem with having a naturally pessimistic frame of mind. In particular, both states produce a feeling of perceived powerlessness that can pervade all aspects of life.

Two approaches to raising self-esteem seem to work well: cognitive behavioral therapy and neurolinguistic programming, NLP for short. Both have the effect of creating a new mental model and hence a new mood. The starting point of both approaches is an acceptance that you are experiencing something unpleasant and that there are things you can do to improve the situation. You need to talk and think about what is on your mind, to try to put into words what you are feeling low about.

Cognitive therapy improves your mood not by working directly on it, but by working on the thoughts that have brought you there. To begin with, it is important to challenge your point of view and see other possible interpretations. Perhaps you are feeling hard done by about a particular job that you applied for and did not get. It may actually be helpful to decide that the interview was unfair and that it was not carried out very well. Or you may have been feeling steadily undermined by your new boss. You may have made certain assumptions about this: for example, that you are no good at your job and that you must be doing things all wrong if your boss feels it necessary to intrude. Or there may be a defect in your superior's character of which you need to be aware. Some therapists go on from here and help you to stop "beating yourself up" about it. By this, they mean that it is counter-productive to waste time blaming yourself when the cause is elsewhere.

Another element of cognitive therapy is the close connection between feelings and thoughts. Interestingly, Susan Greenfield, in *The Private Life of the Brain*, puts feelings at the center of consciousness and what it means to develop your mind. This is a long way

from the old division associated with Descartes and his famous saying, "I think therefore I am." For someone experiencing low self-
esteem, "I feel therefore I am" will be much more helpful, validating
as it does the emotional reality of their situation.

Brain science increasingly seems to support this view. For
some people, music helps at this stage. Music can lift the mood or
perhaps support and draw it out. It depends on individual taste and
mood.

One of the most powerful ways of improving the way you feel
about yourself is through the support you can receive from friends
and loved ones, who, in Maslow's terms, can make you feel that you
"belong." Choosing to spend time with people who make you feel
good about yourself is an important decision. As a result of starting
to think differently about things, you begin also to feel differently
about yourself and your mood changes for the better. You have
changed your mental model of the world.

The second approach, NLP, was the idea of linguist John
Grinder and mathematician Richard Bandler. It draws ideas from a
number of disciplines and combines them. NLP involves increasing
awareness of the way your mind processes experiences—the
"neuro"—being aware of how the way you use language affects the
way you see things—the "linguistic"—and creating new models or
ways of doing things—the "programming."

A key concept in NLP is the idea that there is no such thing
as failure, only feedback. This is an uplifting and important element
of learning to learn more effectively. Not surprisingly, an NLP
approach to improving self-esteem would involve reprogramming
your feelings so that you do not see a setback as a failure.

NLP is always looking for a positive slant on behavior. So, as
part of NLP, it will be important for you to take clear positive steps
toward sorting out whatever it is you have decided is the cause of
you feelings and affirming how you feel at each stage. Using sentences beginning "I can…" and "I am…" works well. Creative visualization is another beneficial technique. You imagine you are an
onlooker observing yourself. In your mind's eye, you rehearse what
it would feel like to achieve your chosen activity. This technique
helps you to learn what it feels like to be competent at something.

LEARNED OPTIMISM AND THE THREE PS

Have you ever wondered why people who seem to be very similarly talented can have very different dispositions toward what needs to be done? Some are "half full" people, always seeing the bright side of a problem, while others are "half empty." Some are only knocked back for a few moments when something goes wrong and rapidly evolve a way of seeing it as an isolated misfortune, while others immediately make it part of a pattern of failure and bad luck.

It is not difficult to imagine which of these two types of people is likely to be more successful, by almost any definition of that word. I expect we all know people in the second category and find them difficult to work with if they happen to be in our team.

Martin Seligman has done more than anyone to illuminate this issue. His key concept of "learned optimism" was developed more than a decade ago and outlined in his book of the same name. Seligman suggests that the world is divided into two kinds of people: optimists and pessimists.

I have no doubt that being successful depends, above all, on being able to learn effectively and releasing your creativity across a broad range of areas of interest. But it is also heavily influenced by whether you are naturally an optimist or can learn to be one.

This concept of optimism is much more fundamental than whether or not you are cheerful or good at thinking positively. It comes out in your reaction to failure. As Seligman puts it, "Changing the destructive things you say to yourself when you experience the setbacks that life deals us is the central skill of optimism." At a time of rapid change, the way you deal with setbacks is, inevitably, of particular importance.

It all comes down to the way you account for things that happen to you, your "explanatory style." Seligman describes this as having three elements: the three Ps of Permanence, Pervasiveness, and Personalization.

Permanence describes whether or not you believe that things always happen to you or that something is an isolated incident. The kind of things you say will give you clues about whether you are naturally optimistic or pessimistic with regard to the permanence of events in your life:

Optimistic

"I'm tired at the moment. After a good night's sleep I'll easily be able to do this"
"My boss is fine unless he's in a bad mood"
"I know that I'm a talented person"
"I can see I didn't do so well on this occasion, but I'll get it right next time"

Pessimistic

"I'll never be able to do this"

"My boss always gives me a hard time"
"I put a lot of effort into doing things"
"You're always telling me I'm not good enough"

Pervasiveness refers to whether you can treat misfortunes as separate phenomena or as failures that will pervade all of your life. The kind of things you say will give you clues about whether you are naturally optimistic or pessimistic with regard to the pervasiveness of events in your life:

Optimistic

"Jim is the kind of salesman who never seems to be honest and open"
"I didn't do so well on this occasion, but there's no reason I can't learn from that"
"I'm good at dealing with people"
"The photocopier's broken down: I'll go down the corridor and try another one"

Pessimistic

"All sales reps are dishonest"

"I am useless"

"I managed to help Bill today"
"Technology and me just don't get along"

Personalization is about whether you feel in control of your life or whether you naturally assume that things happen to you. The kind of things you say will give you clues about whether you are naturally optimistic or pessimistic with regard to the personalization of events in your life:

Optimistic

"I pulled it off"
"I can take control of this situation and do something really good"
"John must have something on his mind"
"What shall we do today?"

Pessimistic

"We managed to do it thanks to their help"
"I am no good at this kind of thing"

"All men are useless"
"I know this is not going to work"

You can find out more about this concept by reading *Learned Optimism: How to Change Your Mind and Your Life*. In particular, Seligman suggests useful ways in which you can develop or learn to be optimistic if you find that you tend toward a pessimistic view of events in your life.

Looking at these examples of things people say, do you think you are an optimist or a pessimist by nature? Are there differences across the three areas of permanence, pervasiveness, and personalization?

One simple thing you can do to change the effect of all the pessimistic statements is to get into the habit of using the past not the present tense. "All men are useless" becomes "Chris was useless (and John may be really helpful tomorrow)." Using the past tense allows you to think about an event as something that happened and is over. You can then move on with more confidence. Try it out yourself. Even just practicing this approach can help.

THE JOINED-UP REVOLUTION

Throughout this book you will find out about the complex connections that exist between mind, body, and spirit. A number of the business leaders I interviewed for this book have testified to the creative benefits of physical exercise, and there is a growing number who attest to the importance of also recognizing a spiritual dimension. In a revolutionary way, they are beginning to make connections across these dimensions of life.

I remember laughing inwardly when I first read the following remark written by James Joyce of one of his characters: "Mr. Duffy lived a short distance from his body."

For more and more people, it is no longer desirable or possible to separate mental, physical, and spiritual matters: they are all interconnected. However, most of us still live too far from our bodies and our hearts. Words like "spirit" are too revolutionary as yet to be included in our business lives.

MENS SANA IN CORPORE SANO

Schools the world over have long sought to develop both mental and physical wellbeing, many of them even using the above quotation from Latin poet Juvenal as their school motto: a healthy mind in a healthy body. In the high street, gyms and fitness centers are now widespread, but much of the business world has been slower to catch on.

As well as keeping you generally healthier, physical exercise—especially aerobic exercise—helps you to relax and to recall things. It reduces stress by triggering the release of endorphins in the brain. At a simple biological level, it sends a burst of oxygenated blood into the brain, so arousing the nervous system generally. According to the Pasteur Institute, exercise stimulates the growth of dendrites and axons, and is, therefore, literally changing the state of your brain.

In an increasingly inactive world of couch potatoes and television, regular exercise has to be one of the most obvious things you can do to improve the state of your mind. And, if you are thinking that personal fitness may be a reasonable goal for individuals, but will never catch on at work in any organized way, consider the following example from one of Britain's leading supermarket chains, Sainsbury's, developed with learning and communications experts Purple Works. It is called the Fit for Life program.

In the past, most attempts to link performance to health and fitness have centered on the reduction of absenteeism. This placed the emphasis on an individual being present at work, rather than focusing on improving their performance.

Sainsbury's Finance Division recently began to explore the idea of creating a work environment that inspires health and fitness. For its director, Hamish Elvidge, this is one of the new challenges for leaders in the twenty-first century. The company has developed an approach that is every bit as much about leadership as it is about health and fitness.

A trial of the 'Fit for Life' program enabled the senior management team to learn enough about the links between fitness and the performance of the brain to make a decision to extend the approach to the whole division.

With Purple Works, they are creating an environment where people can experiment, learn, and decide for themselves why they want to take part, rather than just investing in facilities or forcing people to participate. The aim is to benefit both the individual and the company.

The program is multifaceted, using practical training sessions, workshops, information on the company intranet, and links to external sources of advice and support. Overall, the Sainsbury's team wants to raise energy levels to enable people to gain a better balance between home and work life and so perform better.

BRAIN GYM

Brain gym was created by Paul Dennison in the US to help young people with learning difficulties, especially dyslexia. Recently, the concept has been developed into a more generally helpful activity for us all. While, of course, you exercise your brain all the time, the idea of brain gym is that by exercising in a certain way you are consciously creating patterns of activity in your brain that may be beneficial to you.

Whenever you are feeling the effects of too much work on the computer, try doing this exercise. Start by writing the infinity symbol (below) on a flipchart. Begin with your felt-tip pen in the center, go anti-clockwise, then clockwise, and so on. Do this a few times and establish a good rhythm. Now try doing it with your eyes only rather than with your pen. Let your eyes trace the shape of the infinity sign for at least five circuits. You may find this quite hard work to begin with.

You can find out more about this in Carla Hannaford's book, *Smart Moves: Why Learning Is Not All in Your Head*, from which I have adapted this idea.

GETTING TO THE SPIRITUAL DIMENSION

Most organizations these days have a mission statement. These curious pieces of "corporate speak" often sound positively evangelical. The desire they express in most cases is, quite understandably, the company's aspiration to be number one or to make the most money. If mission statements provide a glimpse of an organization's soul, you would be forgiven for thinking that most businesses are pretty soulless places.

With the dot-com revolution and the growth of communications companies, it has become common for groups of individuals to leave one large company to set up another that has values with which they feel more comfortable. Partly as a result of this and partly, I suspect, out of genuine concern for their people, an increasing number of organizations are beginning to think about the kind of values they would like most to promote among their staff. If retaining good people involves respecting their spiritual interests, this becomes a business rather than a personal issue.

Following the publication of *SQ: The Ultimate Intelligence*, by Danah Zohar and Ian Marshall, a serious attempt has been made to explore the scientific basis for spiritual intelligence and define this new area of interest.

For me, spiritual intelligence is about the capacity to make meaning. It is, as Zohar puts it, the "soul's intelligence." It is linked to the capacity to see lives in wholes, not fragments, and to regenerate ourselves. Most importantly, it is connected to the ability to challenge whether we want to play by the rules of the situation in which we find ourselves. So, a person with a well-developed SQ may not make a business decision on financial grounds alone, preferring to be guided by an ethical viewpoint. Or they may choose not to do something a competitor is doing if there are any concerns about the morality of the action.

Zohar disagrees with the view of the seventeenth-century philosopher John Locke: "All ideas come from sensation or reflection. Let us suppose the mind to be, as we say, white paper, devoid of characters, without ideas." She argues that to understand spiritual intelligence, we need to understand consciousness. Some interesting scientific underpinnings are cited for SQ, mainly from the work of Denis Pare and Rodolfo Llinas. Zohar argues that the brain waves recently discovered—gamma waves oscillating about 40 times a second—may contain the clues to a kind of hyperthinking that is the basis of a higher-order SQ.

Author and ex-Fleet Street editor Will Hutton is quite clear about the role of this kind of intelligence:

I am a very anchored person in a value system. I know who I am. I have also felt that I stand here and can do no other than my values dictate. I will happily live with the consequences.

Hilary Cropper is similarly aware of this dimension. She talks of one of the Indian companies in her FI Group as "a being with a life of its own, with a distinctly spiritual feel." She believes that if you embody spiritual concepts in the way you manage an organization, you will have greater richness and depth.

The practical message you may want to take from this is a wake-up call to examine your values and beliefs and how they fit with your work.

Here are a number of ways of thinking about the values of your current organization:

1 Think of the things that happen on a daily basis that make you really uncomfortable, the traumas of business life. Think, too, of the elements of your professional life that make you feel good, proud to be working for the organization.

Use the chart below to help you group these together and start to come up with words that capture the values that the behaviors you describe exemplify.

Things making me uncomfortable	Values they show	Things I am proud of	Values they show

2 Write down as many words describing values or suggesting ways of behaving as you can think of, starting with the letter A, then B, and so on. For example:

Autocratic
Bullying
Caring

With which of these do you most strongly identify?

3 What saying or line from a song most sums up your approach to life, your values? What line most sums up the values of the place in which you work? Do they sit happily together?

A NEW SIXTH SENSE?

Polynesian thinking has at its heart the idea that to be healthy we need to find and embrace the sacred in life. This involves injecting joy into our lives, what Dr. Paul Pearsall calls "aloha" based on the phonetic representation of the Polynesian word. It is connected with the capacity to be content, patient, kind, and unassuming. It unlocks our ability to be quieter in our lives. For me, this is a more attractive sixth sense than the example of psychic awareness that is sometimes cited as a candidate. We see, we hear, we touch, we smell, we taste—and we are.

As Carl Rogers puts it in *Freedom to Learn*:

Significant learning combines the logical and the intuitive, the intellect and the feelings, the concept and the experience, the idea and the meaning.

GETTING READING TO LEARN—IN A NUTSHELL

YOU HAVE LEARNED:

✔ how to check your own emotional readiness
✔ about the relationship between curiosity and learning
✔ how to read your moods
✔ about the impact of stress on performance
✔ about different kinds of emotional needs
✔ about the importance of self-esteem and some ways of raising it
✔ about the concept of learned optimism and how to become more optimistic
✔ about the relationship between physical fitness and the mind
✔ about a range of emotional responses
✔ how to think about values

KEY IDEAS
Hierarchy of needs
Curiosity
Self-esteem
Cognitive therapy
NLP
Learned optimism
Brain gym
Emotional intelligence
Spiritual intelligence

KEY TECHNIQUES/
APPROACHES
Employee development
Being honest with yourself
Understanding how to deal with what goes wrong
Using the past tense rather than generalizations
Staying physically fit
Using a mood meter
Keeping a feelings diary
Understanding your values

3

Switching On Your Mind

W E ARE, OF COURSE, ALREADY WIRED UP FOR LEARNING. SITTING ON A bus, standing in a queue, watching an argument, struggling with a new computer application—we learn things all the time without really realizing it. Our mind is permanently "wired up" to learn and it is continually processing new experiences.

However, being wired up is not the same thing as being switched on. We may have a good understanding of how our mind works, be emotionally ready, and have the ideal learning environment (see later in this chapter), but if we are not determined to act, all our preparations will be in vain. Even if you are emotionally ready to learn, you have to actively engage your mind to get the best out of life.

You need, as Charles Handy puts it, to cultivate a particular kind of selfishness:

Proper, responsible selfishness, involves a purpose and goal. It is that goal which pulls out the energy to move the wheel. Diminish that goal, displace it, or worst of all, disallow it and we remove all incentive to learn or to change.

Not surprisingly, we all have different reasons for wanting to learn. And in an age where lifelong learning is becoming increasingly significant, knowing more about our motivation to learn is very important. Interestingly, it is only recently that we have begun to understand more about what turns us on to and off from learning. The Campaign for Learning was one of the first organizations in the world to undertake research into this subject and has subsequently helped to persuade the British government to gather this kind of national data regularly in large-scale annual opinion polls.

In its 1998 survey, the Campaign asked individuals how they thought learning could be most useful to them personally. The results give a clear indication of what might switch us on:

	%
Helping me to achieve what I want out of life	17
Satisfying my personal curiosity	12
Improving my job prospects	10
Improving my quality of life	10
Stretching my brain	10
Increasing my self-confidence	7
Improving performance in current job	6
Increase salary	5
Improving my standard of living	5

Source: *Attitudes to Learning*, MORI, 1998

This is an interesting mixture of personal, social, and economic or work-related reasons, but the most significant ones given are personal, about realizing individual potential. It is a central argument of *Power Up Your Mind* that learning to learn involves learning to develop the full range of your intelligences in your work and in your personal life.

The Campaign for Learning also asked people to say which phrase would be most likely to switch them on. The two most popular were:

	%
Discover the talents within you	41
Learn now for a better future	32

When we probed further and asked working adults what would encourage them to learn something related to their work, the following were preferred:

	%
There's more to your job than people realize: get your skills recognized, get qualified	41
Learn more, earn more	36
Learning pays	35

Learndirect, a major British online learning initiative, has subsequently adopted the idea of discovering your hidden talents within as its trademark slogan after much independent research.

What turns you on to learning? Do you agree with these phrases? If not, what would you prefer?

UNDERSTANDING YOUR FUNDAMENTAL DRIVES

You have already read about Maslow's view of our basic emotional needs and how these have to be satisfied in a logical hierarchy. If you now move on from this basic view of human nature, there are a number of important ideas that it will help you to grasp.

The first of these continues to explore the idea of basic needs but goes deeper into the recesses of our motivation. It draws on thinking from the science of communications. John Grant is a successful advertiser and one of the co-founders of the award-winning agency St Luke's. He is also one of the inventors of a new kind of marketing that assumes that people are intelligent and learn! In his book, *The New Marketing Manifesto: The 12 Rules for Building Successful Brands in the 21st Century*, he argues that to understand the motivation to buy, we need to understand 16 fundamental human drives. These are, in alphabetical order:

Avoiding distress	Physicality
Citizenship	Power
Curiosity	Prestige
Family	Sex
Honor	Social acceptance
Hunger	Social contact
Independence	Spirituality
Order	Vengeance

It is interesting to examine these basic driving instincts from the perspective of what motivates us to learn. If you work down the list of drives, you might conclude that some people avoid learning because of the distress they associate with it. Many will see community learning activities, helping with a local club, or clearing up a park as a chance to become more active citizens. Curiosity, as you have already seen, is a major element of being ready to learn—and so on.

Each person will have a different association and their motivation is likely to be affected accordingly.

What about you? Look at the chart below. A few of the words describing basic drives have been filled in. Most have been left blank. Which of these drives are important to you in your decisions to learn? Go through the 16 drives and honestly apply them to your own life.

EFFECT ON MOTIVATION		
Potentially positive	**Potentially neutral**	**Potentially negative**
		Avoiding distress
Curiosity		
Family	Family	Family
		Hunger
		Power
Prestige		
Spirituality		

These powerful driving forces affect all of our lives. They help to determine what we buy and how we spend our time. They are particularly interesting when applied to your learning, because learning is so personal.

Choosing to learn is not the same as choosing to buy a new sofa or a different car. It relates much more intimately to the most important "brand" of all, yourself. How you see yourself and how you feel about this is thus of particular importance.

REWARDING YOUR OWN LEARNING

Albert Einstein tellingly pointed out the dangers of rewards when he said, "Our theories determine what we measure." In other words, we only reward or value what our theories tell us are important. In the business arena, this means that MBAs and professional qualifications are rewarded, while learning about social or emotional intelligence is much less valued.

Few organizations have yet realized that if they want adaptable, flexible employees, they should have reward systems that value those who display these attributes or who can learn effectively.

In too many businesses, learning to learn is not rewarded. Yet, if learning is the single most potent form of sustainable competitive advantage in the Knowledge Age, it is surely what should be being measured and rewarded. A few businesses have begun to appreciate that this is the way forward. In the 1990s, there was some particularly exciting work led by companies like Skandia in Sweden. To accompany its traditional annual reports, Skandia produces a detailed analysis of its intangible assets, the value of its people, the company's reputation, and its customer and supplier networks. An analysis like this examines and puts a value on the kinds of things that learning brings to a business: the knowledge of its customer base and its potential, the capability for innovation and creativity within the organization, and its human capital—the levels of competence and potential of the Skandia workforce.

Another Swedish company, Celemi, has gone a stage further and produced a useful tool to help companies work out their own human capital value, the Celemi Intangible Assets Monitor. Celemi puts this into practice in its own business, reporting on progress as part of its annual accounts. Central to its thinking is the idea that people learn by undertaking challenging projects and that this growth in capacity or intelligence or competence to learn should be recognized.

How to reward yourself

At a personal level, the issue of rewards is complex. Most theorists focus on the distinction between intrinsic and extrinsic rewards for learning. An example of an intrinsic reward is the pleasure it might give you to learn a musical instrument or the good feelings created when you learn how to control your anger. An example of an extrinsic reward would be your child being given a sweet after they have finished their homework or you receiving a degree in return for years of study. The general view is that for learning to be really successful, the learner has to be intrinsically motivated, although it is clear that having external positive feedback is also bound to be helpful.

One of the best-known thinkers in this area of motivation is Frederick Herzberg. Writing in the 1960s about attitudes to work, he established a helpful distinction between hygiene factors and satisfiers. If you think of this in terms of food, Herzberg's distinction becomes clearer. Food may be carefully prepared and technically safe to eat. These are hygiene factors. Alternatively, it can be deliciously tasty, from an organic source, and very nutritious. These would be satisfiers. Herzberg showed how the analogy holds good for motivation at work.

However, the real value of Herzberg's approach lies in his development of the distinction between intrinsic and extrinsic motivation. He points out that the opposite of being demotivated is *not* being motivated, it is not *being demotivated*. You can minimize the dissatisfaction by creating hygiene factors, but you need things that will really satisfy a learner to make them motivated. You can see this expressed below:

Switched off from learning	←	→	Not switched off from learning
Not switched off from learning	←	→	Switched on to learning

If you stop being switched off from learning, it just means that you stop being against it. It doesn't mean that you are *for* it! Many people who go on training courses at work reluctantly get themselves into a position of being not switched *off*, but they don't go further and become switched *on* to the learning they are being offered.

Once you understand this strange kind of layering of opposites, you are much better equipped to motivate yourself and others to learn. You need to be really "satisfied" if you are going to be switched on and, therefore, powered up to learn.

Sometimes external rewards can even work against you. For example, it has been found that if you are trying to encourage children to read, rewarding them for the number of books they read may in fact be counter-productive. Apparently, if you do this they will read a higher number of books at speed, but not enjoy, learn, or remember what they have read.

Nevertheless, most of us are able to work out how to administer treats as rewards when we have done something we have set our mind to. Such rewards might be going for a walk, a weekend break away, a meal out with our partner, or simple things such as a cup of coffee or a piece of chocolate (although for the effects of certain foods on your brain, don't forget what you read earlier!). But, remember this. If you come to depend on external rewards, what happens when you stop receiving them? Do you go on or do you grind to a halt because you lack the internal drive?

Think about the learning you have done in your life so far. How much of it was motivated by extrinsic rewards and how much did you undertake because you wanted to do it for its own sake? Of the things you are currently thinking about learning, how many are you actively switched on to rather than not switched off from? What kind of rewards work best for you?

A FORMULA FOR MOTIVATION TO LEARN

When you were at school, the learning you were offered was probably broad and diverse in its content and style. If you ever asked why you were learning something, unless you had one of those special teachers who took the trouble to relate the learning to your needs, the answer you were probably given was a version of "just in case" or "because it's in the syllabus." Consequently, you learned things that you have probably never used since. In some cases that may have felt wonderful. For example, some people recall learning Latin with great pleasure, even though it has only enabled them to be a little more certain now about the meaning of certain French or Spanish words. Others might say that they did not enjoy and have found no subsequent use for the ancient languages they learned at school. It is all a matter of opinion.

In today's world and as an adult lifelong learner, you will probably be much more likely to adopt a "just in time" approach, learning things as and when you need to.

I want to suggest a way of looking at motivation to learn. In developing this, I have been particularly influenced by two British researchers, Andrea Spurling and Jim Smith, authors of *Lifelong Learning: Riding the Tiger*, through working with them on research into this area for the Campaign for Learning. Consider the following formula:

$$R + V + P + I = M$$

- ◆ R is the amount of readiness to learn, as described in Chapter 2.
- ◆ V is the anticipated value of the learning. This could be financial, social, or cultural.
- ◆ P is the probability of the learning being successful. This will depend on previous experience, on your perceived effectiveness as a learner, on the degree to which the learning you are being offered matches your learning style, and on your likely ability to overcome any barriers along the way.
- ◆ I is the likely impact of the learning on your life. This could be in terms of the opportunities it will create, the likelihood of dealing with some external change, or the degree to which, if you can acquire the learning, you will be markedly more fulfilled as an individual.
- ◆ M is the amount of motivation you have toward a particular learning opportunity.

So, if you were really ready to learn, if what you were planning to learn was extremely valuable to you, if you thought you were likely to be able to do it, and if you also thought that the learning might significantly improve your life, you would be well motivated.

In reality, you will feel different degrees of motivation about different learning options. You certainly do not go round calculating this mathematically; nor should you. But, if you are serious about becoming a competent learner, you may find this formula useful. It may at least help you to explain why you are feeling motivated or not. The formula also gives you a way of working out the relevance of the learning to your particular life stage.

Or, to put another way, it determines the WIIFM factor, the "What's in it for me?" element. This is Charles Handy's "proper selfishness" in the quotation at the start of this chapter.

Apply the motivation formula to something that you are thinking of learning. What does it tell you about your motivation? Use the chart below to help you do this:								
Readiness	+	Value	+	Probability	+	Impact	=	Motivation

Put ticks or a rating out of ten under each of the first four headings and then see how many ticks or how close your number is to 40 in the last box.

MOTIVATION AND THE MIND

So far, I have looked at some of the important theories of motivation and tried to provide the context in which learning activity takes place. Let's recap on what you know so far about how the mind works in this area.

You have learned about the mind's natural tendency to explore and to make connections and patterns. You have seen why it performs less well when it is under undue stress. You are aware that diet, health, and the amount of sleep you have had all affect your motivation and ability to sustain learning. You have learned about the importance of being emotionally ready, primed to accept new data, and about the mind's tendency to interpret events differently, depending on whether you are optimistic or motivated.

While much of this is common sense, the importance of biological and psychological factors in learning is too often underestimated.

GETTING THE BIG PICTURE

Brain science is also important for motivation. We touched on some of the ideas when you "unpacked" your brain in Chapter 1, but I want to explore them in a little more detail. Your brain learns by processing experiences. Its neurons are continually trying to make connections between each other and so establish pathways, embedding memories and knowledge in your mind. With so much sensory data, it is easy to see that your brain needs to be able to make sense of it all. It needs to focus its energies and it needs to engage and connect. It likes to find and make patterns. It likes to have the big picture and then to be able to create patterns or connections within this. Being motivated to learn something or focusing on something specific helps your mind to create patterns. It enables it to find the connections between data it already has and new data it is acquiring.

For learning to be fast and effective, your brain needs to be given the big picture first.

It is a bit like solving a jigsaw puzzle. You need to see the whole picture, probably by looking at what is on the lid of the box, before the fragments of colored wood make any sense. Then, you need to break a sea of differently shaped pieces into smaller groups. You might start by picking all the bits with a straight edge. If it is an outdoor scene, you might select all those with blue sky on them. If there is a building with a large area of pattern or color, you might select this as a group, and so on. Your brain likes to work in a similar way. When it is allowed to, it can be much more effective.

It is the same with motivating yourself to learn. You need the big picture—your overall goal and how this fits into your life—and you need to be able to break this up into manageable pieces.

BALANCING CHALLENGE AND THREAT

You have learned how your "primitive" or "reptilian" brain reacts if it is put under too much pressure. At its simplest, it interprets any input as potentially life threatening and decides whether to run away or stay and fight. In fact, the ideal state seems to be a combination of curiosity, relaxation, and alertness, which you can read more about when exploring creativity in Chapter 9.

Your brain needs challenge and stimulation. Challenge makes your neurons connect, encouraging them to grow more dendrites until every avenue of a problem has been explored. You need challenge, but not too much of it. In terms of your motivation, it is important, therefore, that your goals are challenging but still attainable. If there is too much challenge or, worse still, too much stress, more primitive instinctive responses cut in, denying you access to key parts of your brain, especially the more complex areas in your limbic system and neocortex.

The impact of stress and challenge on your motivation is as follows:

	High threat	Low threat
High challenge	Feel controlled and compelled	Feel engaged
Low challenge	Feel controlled and demotivated	Feel bored

You are most likely to be motivated if you are in a high-challenge, low-threat environment. Ideally, this also contains many opportunities for you to receive and give feedback on your progress. It is true that it is perfectly possible to learn in each of the other three quadrants. Indeed, under high stress extraordinary results have been produced. But, it may have a cost to you as an individual. And, unless your goals are set and owned by you, it is unlikely that your motivation to learn will be sustainable.

How challenged you feel will, of course, depend on how competent you are. A high-performing chief executive might show signs of great stress if you asked them to sing an operatic aria on stage!

Looking at the connection between challenge and competence can also be helpful:

	Low skills	High skills
High challenge	Feel anxious	Feel stimulated
Low challenge	Feel safe and unstimulated	Feel bored

These two diagrams will help you to work out the probability of being successfully motivated in your learning.

10 ways to boost your motivation

However good you are at motivating yourself, there will always be times when your motivation flags. Here are some other ways in which you can revive it and the reasons these are likely to work:

1   *Give yourself a reward.* This will make you feel good, confirming your achievements so far and making you want to continue.
2   *Stop what you are doing and take some physical exercise.* Your brain needs lots of oxygenated blood to work well. Just standing up releases an extra 20 percent. Taking some exercise will help you to stop fretting about things and relax. You may even find that you solve your problem while you are exercising.
3   *Take a break.* Unless you are completely "in the flow," most people find that a few minutes' break every 20 or 30 minutes refreshes the mind without losing your engagement in the activity. A change of environment often helps you to see things differently.
4   *Check that you have got the big picture.* Your brain is continually trying to make connections, so giving the big picture in advance gives it time to make sense of things and "gather" all it knows about the subject.

5   *Work out a different way of breaking up what you are learning into smaller chunks*. Your brain finds it easier to deal with big issues when they are broken down into smaller elements.

6   *Try getting the information in a different way*. Use a different mode, perhaps adopting a visual or physical mode if you have been listening for a long time. By doing this, you will be bringing a different part of your brain to bear on the matter. Visualizing what success would look like may help you.

7   *Celebrate what you have done so far*. Thinking positively about your achievements is likely to help you to want to go on. Making a list of all the things you are pleased about will help.

8   *Find something to laugh about*. There is evidence that when you laugh your brain releases endorphins, which act as relaxants.

9   *Ask a friend or member of your family for help*. Two minds are better than one!

10   *Stop and think what you did last time you felt like this*. Make a list of all the ways you have dealt with this kind of situation before. The brain loves patterns and by doing this you may help it to make a new connection.

THE IMPORTANCE OF WHERE YOU LEARN

Most of us start our learning journeys in the home with our family. We visit a library, a museum, a town center, a leisure attraction, or a stately home with them. We watch television and go to the cinema. Then, when we reach a certain age, we go to school. After this college and, perhaps, university beckon. At some stage, we start earning a living and learning on and off the job. Throughout our lives we travel and meet new people.

How you learn and how you feel about learning will probably depend on where you are. For example, many people feel that they are a very different person at work from the one they are at home. How does this affect our readiness to learn? Clearly, for much of our lives, we have no choice about where we are learning: we are either at school, at work, or at home. Yet, we are potentially learning wherever we are.

The Campaign for Learning has gathered interesting data about the different environments where people would prefer to learn. In answer to the question "In which three of the following places do you think you personally learn most?", we received the following responses:

	%
Home	57
Work	43
Libraries	36
College/university	29
On holidays/traveling	22
Museums	13
Adult learning centers	13
At school	11

Source: Campaign for Learning, *Attitudes to Learning*, MORI poll, 1998

It is interesting that the two places in which most people learn are their own home and their workplace.

What about you? Where do you like to learn? Does this list hold true for you? How much chance to you have to learn at work? Do you learn in different ways depending on where you are?

WHO YOU LEARN WITH

There is more to environment, of course, than merely place. It is also about the other people who use it.

Human beings are social animals. Some of us choose to live on our own, but the vast majority live in groups of two or more. Even those who select privacy for their domestic arrangements seek contact with other human beings throughout their lives. Not surprisingly, much of our learning is informal and social. It depends on the presence of other people.

This has been true from our earliest days, both as individuals and as a species. Babies learn from their mother, their father, and their family and friends. They watch and listen and imitate. Eventually, they hear a word, say it, say it again, and make a pattern out of the saying. Learning is an integral part of our social way of life. Similarly, in the earliest times, men and women lived in caves and simple shelters. They only had each other to learn from about birth, death, sexual maturity, killing and curing animals, and harvesting plants that would not poison them.

For many of us, who we learn with largely determines the way we will be learning. And while we are social creatures, we also like to be private.

In our survey, we asked: "In which three of the following ways do you prefer to learn?" Responses were as follows:

	%
Through doing practical things	45
Alone/self-study	45
With a group being given instruction	33
Exchanging information with others	32
Practicing alone	27
Watching demonstrations	24
Thinking for yourself	22
One-to-one study with a tutor	21
Facilitated group activities	20

Source: Campaign for Learning, *Attitudes to Learning*, MORI poll, 1998

Are you a social learner or do you prefer to learn alone? Do you like to be taught or to find out for yourself? Do you enjoy group work or would you rather work at your own pace?

GETTING YOUR LEARNING ENVIRONMENT READY

Before you embark on any period of concentrated learning, it is worth taking stock of your immediate environment.

If you were getting ready for a holiday, you would be thinking about the clothes to take and the equipment you needed, and beginning to imagine yourself in the environment you had chosen to visit. You need to exercise at least the same care over your own learning, wherever it happens.

You should think carefully about the kind of environment that makes you feel both emotionally secure and intellectually stimulated.

Most of the questions below apply at home, although you probably have even more factors to consider, not least of which is what the rest of your family or friends are doing.

If you are learning at work, do you like to be sitting alongside a colleague, round a table, in a classroom situation, taking part in operational activities, going off to a hotel to reflect?
Do you like a noisy or a quiet atmosphere?
Do you like background music? Do you find that music helps to tune in your mind?
Do you like to be in a well-lit area or working under low light?
Do you like to be sitting at a desk? Walking around? Sitting on an easy chair? Lying on the floor or on a cushion?
Do you prefer early starts or sessions after work?
Do you like to have posters around you with key images or sayings?
Do you have evidence of your own success that you could display in your chosen environment?
How warm do you like to be?

It is also important to make sure that you have the right equipment around you. Use the following checklist as a starting point and add your own preferred items to it:

- ✔ *Water*
- ✔ *Post-it notes*
- ✔ *Other colored adhesive strips of paper*
- ✔ *Large pieces of paper*
- ✔ *Colored paper*
- ✔ *Voice recording machine of some kind*
- ✔ *Laptop computer*
- ✔ *Access to the internet*
- ✔ *Highlighter pens*
- ✔ *Felt-tip pens*
- ✔ *Index cards*
- ✔ *Posters with quotations*
- ✔ *Posters with pictures*
- ✔ *Reference books*
- ✔ *Paperclips*
- ✔ *Stapler and staples*
- ✔ *Hole punch*

✔   *Range of folders*
✔   *Range of clear plastic wallets*
✔   *Any equipment specific to what you are learning*

What else do you like to have with you?

These suggestions may seem obvious, but I am surprised at how often people I work with simply have not thought about some of the most basic equipment for their learning. I am sure you will want to add many other items to this list.

THE PRESSURES OF LIFE

There have been some interesting changes in patterns of social life over the last few decades. It used to be common for one parent only to work; now more than half of families have both parents in employment. And, of course, the working week has grown insidiously from a reasonable 40 hours to an elastic 50 or 60.

Televisions, computers, computer games, and mobile phones have come to dominate many homes. Watching television is the core ritual for many families, where having breakfast and supper together and playing family games were dominant rituals in the past. While most people once knew and trusted their neighbors, today we are likely not to know them and to be worried about the noise they make. This is not a lament for the past, but a reminder of the social context in which learning sits.

A key issue for you when you try to set aside time for learning at home, at work, or anywhere else is your ability to create an environment where you can be free from real-world intrusions. This is as important for the adult learner as it is for a teenager struggling to complete their homework.

How do you manage this in your family social life?

OVERCOMING BARRIERS TO LEARNING

You are ready to learn, feeling relaxed and alert. You have decided where you want to learn and have organized your learning environment. But, somehow you never seem to get round to it—learning that new computer program, working out how to tile your bathroom, finding out why your tomato plants produce fruit that never ripen. What's the problem? Your mind is receptive but still not turned on.

As with horses, so with learners. You can take us to water but you cannot make us drink. As US academic Chris Argyris puts it: "No one can develop anyone else apart from himself. The door to development is locked from inside."

This is the conundrum of being motivated to learn. Once you have left school or college, all of life's conflicting demands press down on you. There are many barriers to prevent you from engaging in learning. Here are some of the common ones, with suggestions of how you can overcome them.

◆   *I haven't got enough time.* If it is important, then you have to make time for it! Set aside small but regular amounts of time to fit in with your other commitments and think about giving yourself whole days or weekends devoted to something you are keen to learn. Use the life planning activity in Chapter 12.

◆   *I can't get the kind of learning I want near where I live or work.* This may be true at first sight, but think more laterally. Can you get it online? Have you really investigated what is available? You need to search a long way beyond the training department of the organization for which you work. In the UK there is a free national helpline, Learndirect on 0800 100900, and other countries have similar ideas. Or try talking to your colleagues and friends about what you want to do and see what creative ideas they come up with. Rather than going on a customer care course, for example, why not go and see how another organization not in your line of work does it?

◆   *What's on offer does not fit with the way I like to learn.* The way you like learning is a helpful first approach when searching for what you want, but will be very limiting if you use it as an excuse for not trying something different! The point about understanding your preferred learning style is that you may want to learn to use and even enjoy other approaches. Nevertheless, saying that you want an active or informal or practical or academic type of learning may also be helpful to you in finding someone who can give you what you want.

◆ *I associate learning with school: being talked at and sitting in rows*. You are not alone. I have met men and women in their sixties whose school days were certainly not the happiest of their life! The good news is that much of the learning you might choose to do today is not like the school experience you may remember.

◆ *Learning really turns me off*. Learning does not have a good image for some people because in their mind they connect the word with education or training, things they are told to do, sometimes against their will. In fact, most of us associate the word learning with discovery and searching out our hidden talents. However, it may well be that you do have to overcome a mental barrier to get started.

◆ *Where I work learning is frowned on*. In too many schools, homes, and workplaces it is not cool to be smart or to learn. This is so despite our love of game shows, quiz games, pub quizzes, and crossword puzzles the world over. While there are cultural variations in this depending on where you live, it may be that you have to accept that not all of your friends or colleagues will immediately see why you are choosing to learn something. You can look forward to telling them about how much you have got from your learning at a later stage.

◆ *My other responsibilities mean that much as I'd like to, I couldn't commit myself to a course*. You may well have real issues to work through. Childcare and family or other care responsibilities are good examples of these. The first step is to decide what it is that you want to do and then work through the options for how you can get help in discharging your other duties to your satisfaction. You certainly won't be in a fit emotional state if you are worrying about someone you care for rather then concentrating on your learning.

◆ *I didn't realize that "doing it yourself" was learning*. You learn so much without realizing that you are doing so. In a typical day, you may pick up many different tips, learn a new skill, do something in your garden or in the community—all these are learning. Often the informal learning is the most valuable and the most real. Congratulate yourself on everything you are already learning.

◆ *I am afraid it might change things.* Learning is powerful stuff! You will almost inevitably be changed by what you learn. It is best to be honest about this possibility and try to share your thoughts and feelings openly. My wife started to learn the piano recently after being told as a child that she was no good at music. She is doing very well. At one level you could say that all she has done is to begin to acquire a new skill. In fact, her success in learning has changed her, boosting her confidence as a learner and releasing a musical talent she had been told she did not have.

◆ *I am too old to learn.* However old you are, this isn't true. While you may have heard the slogan "Use it or lose it," what we know about our brains does not support this. It is true that your brain cells gradually die off as you get older, but what is more important is that even with only half your brain cells intact, you have more neural capacity than you need. It is true that if you don't seek actively to use your brain you may get a little "rusty," but this is really about the patterns of connections between your brain cells rather than the number of cells. It is common sense that if you stop using or practicing a skill you will be a little slower. More positively, there is growing evidence that learning makes you healthier in later years. Some doctors in the UK have even begun prescribing learning rather than drugs, with very encouraging results!

◆ *I couldn't possibly expose myself in front of my boss or those who work for me.* A fear of failure or lack of success is the reason that some very senior executives find it difficult to accept the challenge to learn to be different, and help explain why coaching and mentoring are such important activities. The same reason can be equally powerful for those in less senior positions. Nine times out of ten, however, those around you end up admiring your determination to see something through, even if they do not immediately give you that impression.

◆ *I am no good at learning and I'll be humiliated in front of other people.* This fear is present to some degree in almost all of us. You were born able to learn. You have done it naturally throughout your life. This book is trying to help you rekindle your appetite for learning. Mentally rehearsing what you are going to do will help, as will equipping yourself with positive statements to use in the event of comments from others.

For all of these examples, it may be helpful to remember that you are learning all the time, you just may not be aware of it. You learn about the way your boss likes to do things by watching. You pick up ways of resolving a conflict by listening to a skilled friend, for example.

Sometimes it is helpful to think back over the last week and try to be more aware of the things that you have learned.

How many of these barriers do you recognize in your life? Think of occasions when you have come up against a similar barrier and remember how you overcame it.

SWITCHING ON YOUR MIND—IN A NUTSHELL

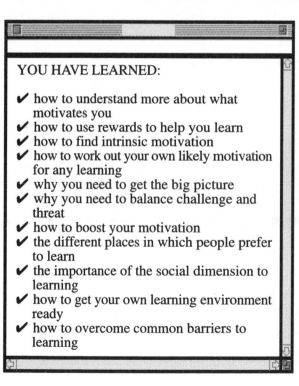

YOU HAVE LEARNED:

✔ how to understand more about what motivates you
✔ how to use rewards to help you learn
✔ how to find intrinsic motivation
✔ how to work out your own likely motivation for any learning
✔ why you need to get the big picture
✔ why you need to balance challenge and threat
✔ how to boost your motivation
✔ the different places in which people prefer to learn
✔ the importance of the social dimension to learning
✔ how to get your own learning environment ready
✔ how to overcome common barriers to learning

KEY IDEAS
Proper selfishness
Intrinsic and extrinsic rewards
Intangible assets
Hygiene factors and satisfiers

KEY TECHNIQUES/ APPROACHES
Getting the big picture
Balancing challenge and threat
Using rewards effectively
Using a range of equipment to support your learning

Part II
Go For It
Becoming a competent learner

COMING UP IN THIS PART

- The idea of learnacy explained
- How to work out your own learning style
- The first three of the five Rs: how to be more resourceful, how to remember more, and how to be more resilient
- The idea of the learning cycle
- How to be more creative and the idea of multiple intelligences
- Why learning pays

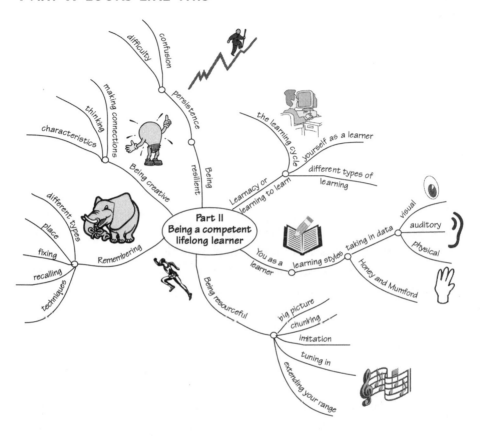

A KEY SENTENCE TO REMEMBER FROM THIS PART

So, think not of the old 3Rs, but of the exciting new 5Rs—Resourcefulness, Remembering, Resilience, Reflectiveness, and Responsiveness. These skills are at the heart of what makes a competent lifelong learner.

A FAMOUS THOUGHT TO CONSIDER

Success in the marketplace increasingly depends on learning, yet most people don't know how to learn.

Chris Argyris

4

Learnacy

W HEN MOST PEOPLE THINK ABOUT LEARNING, THEY THINK THEMSELVES
straight into the thick of a learning experience. But you know better! You have seen how your mind needs to be powered up before
you start learning. You know you have to have a broader understanding of learnacy, or how you learn to learn.

Let's suppose that you are ready and switched on to learn.
How can you improve the way you use your mind? How can you
ensure that you become a competent learner? Now that you understand the basic information about your brain and why it is easy to
waste your effort if you are not in the right frame of mind and eager
to start, this part of the book contains a few of the answers and
some of the key techniques.

And when you have finished this part, "Go For It," turn to
Part III. Just as it was important to get ready beforehand, so it is
essential that you get steady, becoming able to change and adapt
the way you do things after you have learned something. In this
way, you will be using your mind more effectively.

It is possible to take a reductionist view of learning that
assumes that it is simply the sum of a few techniques and skills.
However, this is clearly not the case. Learning is complex, slippery
stuff. As you will have seen from the earlier chapters, the techniques
are only a small part of the story. If learning were an iceberg, then
the techniques would be the visible bit above the surface. What lies
below the water, the emotional and psychological self-
understanding that we have been exploring and the areas still to
come, would be the solid bulk of the ice hidden from most people's
sight. You will see how this is the case when I explain, on page 82,

that the old "3Rs" that many of us grew up with at school are no longer as relevant in today's world. In particular, you will see how two of the new "5Rs," Reflecting and Responsiveness, come *after* what is normally thought of as learning, and are dealt with in Part III.

Once you come to that moment when you are consciously ready to start learning, when you realize that you want to do something but can't, you need to go through a number of stages to achieve competency in your chosen area.

Take the example of driving a car. To begin with, you do not even know that you want to learn how to drive a car. Then, you become conscious that you can't do something you want to do. Perhaps as a teenager you watched one of your parents driving and begun to wonder what it would be like. Or you had an elder brother or sister who seemed to be having more fun than you because they knew how to drive.

So, you learn how to do it but remain very conscious of how you undertake every aspect of the task, painfully looking in the mirror, signaling, and then maneuvering out into the road in a very mechanical way and going forward and backward as you attempt to reverse the car into a small parking space. Finally, you can do everything without even being aware of what you are doing. You can drive along changing gear, instinctively looking in your mirror from time to time and chatting as you do so.

In other words, you have gone full circle from not being aware that you were an incompetent driver to being competent, so skilled that you don't even notice what you are doing. Most commentators agree that the process looks like this:

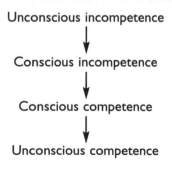

Unconscious incompetence

↓

Conscious incompetence

↓

Conscious competence

↓

Unconscious competence

This process is at the heart of learnacy and learning to learn. Recently, Dr. Peter Honey and I have set about trying to work out what the key skills of learning to learn are.

As far as we know, no one has systematically tried to explore and define this area, despite growing interest in it. To do so, we asked a number of people interested in learning what they thought were the key elements of this big and difficult concept. Then, we conducted a survey among a much larger group and asked them to rank the elements in order of importance. The results were fascinating. Respondents told us that the 30 listed below were either critical or very important to them:

Rank	Description	%
1	Identifying how much of your learning is solitary and how much collaborative	85.9
2	Choosing to learn online	85.3
3	Using media or books about learning	85.3
4	Planning to use a particular medium and then trying it out	84.1
5	Consciously modeling or imitating others	82.4
6	Distinguishing between formal and informal learning experiences	81.8
7	Keeping a written record of your learning	81.8
8	Practicing or strengthening underutilized styles	81.8
9	Identifying how much of your learning is passive versus active	81.2
10	Finding out how other people learn	81.2
11	Breaking learning into a series of "hows"	80.6
12	Continually seeking to add new learning techniques to your repertoire from all possible sources	80.0
13	Identifying how much of your learning is absorbing facts or information versus experiences or trial and error	80.0
14	Persisting with new learning methods or techniques until they become easier	80.0
15	Habitually exploring how you learn	78.8
16	Pondering the different feelings, pleasant and unpleasant, triggered by different learning experiences	78.2
17	Focusing on developing your preferred learning style(s)	77.6
18	Experimenting, on a trial and error basis, with different ways of learning	77.6
19	Deliberately choosing challenging learning options	77.6
20	Using mind maps or spider diagrams	75.9
21	Consciously using a learning model, for example, the learning cycle or the idea of multiple intelligences	75.9
22	Pondering your motives for learning, the original ones and the ones that keep you going	75.9
23	Using techniques to activate your memory	74.4
24	Using a variety of study skills or techniques	74.7

Rank	Description	%
25	Understanding the different roles played by people when learning together	74.1
26	Getting in touch with the feelings or emotions that suffuse learning	72.4
27	Answering the question, "How can I improve the way that I learn?"	72.4
28	Learning from people who do it differently	70.0
29	Accepting accidental, unplanned experiences and working out how they contribute to your learning	70.0
30	Undertaking activities to strengthen learning skills and/or overcome weaknesses	70.0

Source: Peter Honey and Bill Lucas

We were surprised at the high level of consensus that this survey showed.

What do you think? Do you agree with this selection? Are there any techniques that you use in developing your own learning that are not listed here? Is there anything on this list that surprised you? How many of these techniques do you feel you have as part of the resources you use as a learner?

If you look at these 30 skills, they fall into three broad categories: understanding yourself as a learner, learning to use new techniques, and learning about learning.

UNDERSTANDING YOURSELF AS A LEARNER

It is entirely to be expected that you will want to know yourself a little better. Examples of useful areas to explore from our survey would include:

◆ Identifying how much of your learning is solitary and how much is collaborative.
◆ Identifying how much of your learning is passive versus active.
◆ Identifying how much of your learning is absorbing new facts or information versus experiential learning.

LEARNING TO USE NEW TECHNIQUES: THE 5RS

So far in this book you have read about a number of new learning techniques, including these "getting ready to learn" skills:

◆   Consciously modeling or imitating others.
◆   Pondering the different feelings—pleasant and unpleasant—triggered by different learning experiences.
◆   Pondering your motives for learning—the original ones and the ones that keep you going.
◆   Understanding the different roles played by people when learning together.
◆   Getting in touch with the emotions that suffuse learning.

Most of the rest of our list are the techniques you need if you are to become an effective learner.

Let me take you back to your school days for a moment. For most of us, the essential tools or basic skills of childhood were the so-called 3Rs: wRiting, aRithmetic, and Reading. While these remain core skills, they are no longer the only ones to acquire in the Knowledge Age.

British academic Guy Claxton has produced a compelling analysis of this issue in *Wise-Up: The Challenge of Lifelong Learning*. Claxton argues for a different set of 3Rs: Resilience, Resourcefulness, and Reflectiveness. These, he asserts, are the new core areas of competence on which the lifelong learner should be concentrating. They are much broader than the old 3Rs. And that is the point—they refer to the real world of lifelong learning, where attitudes and skills are much more important than the possession of specific knowledge.

I agree with him. But, there are two further very important areas: Remembering and Responsiveness. Memory is the key to so much of our learning, especially memory for techniques and approaches rather than memory for facts. In an electronic age, this latter attribute is increasingly far less important. And it is the capacity to adapt that is the real attribute lifelong learners need if they are to be able to change the way they do things in their lives.

So, don't think of the old 3Rs, but of the exciting new 5Rs: Resourcefulness, Remembering, Resilience, Reflectiveness, and Responsiveness. These skills are at the heart of what makes a competent lifelong learner.

Resourcefulness, Remembering, and Resilience are dealt with in Part II, while Reflectiveness and Responsiveness are explored in detail in Part III, as they tend to come after a learning experience.

LEARNING ABOUT LEARNING

If you accept the idea that learnacy is as important as numeracy and literacy, it is natural to want to find out more about learning theory.

The most obvious way of learning about learning in general is reading books or using other media to find out about the subject. Reading a book such as *Power Up Your Mind* is a good example, as is watching a television program about how your brain works, or using a CD-Rom to find out about learning styles. Earlier in this chapter, I explored the idea that learning is a progression from unconscious incompetence to unconscious competence via conscious incompetence and conscious competence. For most people, the stage when you become consciously competent is the most important one, hence the subtitle of this part of the book. So, if you are interested in getting the best out of your mind, you will want to read about the subject generally. You have already encountered theories that could be useful to you.

In our list there are two obvious examples:

◆ distinguishing between formal and informal learning, and
◆ understanding the different roles played by people learning together.

It is a paradox of learning to learn that it is difficult to allow your interest to remain at a theoretical level. In this sense, it is quite different from learning about, say, architecture. You might learn about how medieval houses were designed but would not necessarily want to rush out and build one. Your interest remains valid without your having to move from the theoretical to the practical. With learning this is less likely to be the case. It may be that until you have experienced something, you have not really internalized it. Reading about learning to learn rather than doing it is inherently likely to be frustrating! It is likely that you will want to apply the insights you have gained to your own life.

> *Pause for a moment and think about the 5Rs in your own learning life. For example, how resilient are you as a learner? Or, put another way, what do you do when the going gets tough? Do you stick with it or do you give up? Do you have strategies for working things through? What about your resourcefulness? Do you take time to reflect on what you have learned? If so, how do you do this?*

THE LEARNING CYCLE

Good gardeners want to learn about the cycle of the seasons. People who love DIY can tell you exactly how to go about doing a particular task. Anyone who has cooked anything knows that you need to have some kind of an idea how you are going to create a meal, even if you are not the sort of person to follow a recipe. The same is, of course, true of learning.

Competent learners tend to want to know a little about the theories underpinning such an important activity. Unfortunately, there have been some very wrong-headed notions attached to learning for far too long. One of the most pernicious of these is IQ, the idea that there is only one way in which you can be clever. Another is sometimes referred to as the "tabula rasa" or "clean slate" view of learning. In this approach, the learner is seen as an empty vessel waiting to be filled up with knowledge. Learners are passive beings waiting for their teachers to teach them. These two ideas have, in my view, poisoned the school systems of the world and given the training departments of so many large organizations a serious illness. The disease they have caught is, of course, the problem of passivity. This is sometimes called "chalk and talk," a strange custom whereby learners are put in rows and spoken at while they diligently copy down what is being said. It is highly inefficient as a method of learning.

Learning is essentially an active experience. One of the first theorists to describe this convincingly was David Kolb, who articulated something called "experiential learning," now widely seen as a model for effective learning. He argued that learning starts from actual experience. It is followed by observations from reflection and leads to the creation of a new model or theory. This is followed, in turn, by active experimentation and further refinement.

For many in the business world, this has a ring of truth to it, following as it does the product development cycle with which many are familiar. The Swedish knowledge expert Klas Mellander goes further still in proposing a development of Kolb's cycle as follows:

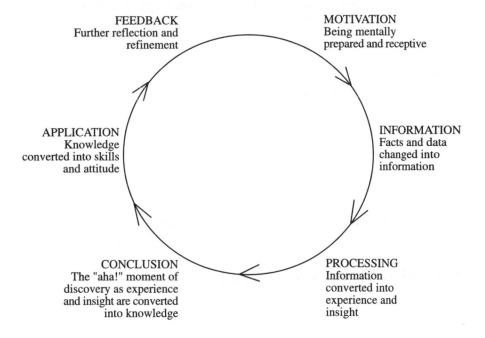

Think about what you have learned in the last month. Have you had some "aha!" moments? If so, what were they? If not, how would you describe the process by which you tend to learn? Does it fit with any of the models we have looked at so far?

For me, the diagram above shows a more realistic description of what is going on when we learn, although if you think that you will always have that "aha!" or "eureka!" moment you are mistaken, as you will see in the next chapter. There certainly are many times when things do suddenly fall into place like this, but on the whole learning is much more messy.

Mellander's model is really helpful in pointing up one of the most powerful ways in which learning helps individuals and organizations to be successful. This is by capturing the tacit and, therefore, hidden knowledge that has been learned, which will be of only limited use unless it can be shared.

Another way of looking at Mellander's model is to think of any experience of learning as having four different stages. I have used the example of making an omelette to illustrate this.

Know what: You recognize an omelette and have eaten one

↓

Know how: You have read a recipe and tried cooking one

↓

Know why: You know why it is important not to get egg shells into the mix and why the butter should not be too hot

↓

Care why: You care about why it is important to have good quality of ingredients and how omelettes fit into a balanced diet

---

See if you could draw a model or diagram of how you think you learn.

DIFFERENT TYPES OF LEARNING

It is very easy to end up thinking so generally about the concept of learning that you fail to notice that there are very different ways of doing it.

Think of a typical working day in your life. Using the chart overleaf, work out how many different types of learning you experience. For each of the categories, see if you can come up with at least one example. Now, think about all of your last month's learning. Can you categorize it using these headings? Are there any others you can think of?

Types of learning

Permanent—dealing with a difficult emotional situation, saying sorry

Disposable—learning a new computer program, assembling a new set of flat-packed shelves

Formal—going to college, taking part in a training course

Informal—watching a colleague you admire handle a meeting, talking about what you thought about a new film with your family

Accredited externally—taking an MBA, gaining a certificate for life saving

For personal interest only—digging a pond in your garden, learning to tile your bathroom

Social—learning to play a team game, working on a new project with a group of colleagues

Individual—reading a book, surfing the web

Compulsory—going to school, going on a training course that you did not choose

Voluntary—deciding to surf the web, learning how to speak French

Many people find that of these ten different categories, "informal" contains the most items. What about you? If you agree, why do you think this is? If not, what was the category into which most of your learning fell?
Could you try and concentrate on a different type of learning over the next month?

LEARNACY—IN A NUTSHELL

YOU HAVE LEARNED:

✔ about conscious and unconscious competence and the learning cycle
✔ about the range of elements that go to make up learnacy
✔ that, to be a competent learner, you need to understand yourself as a learner, learn to use new techniques, and continue to learn about learning
✔ that learning is a process of experience
✔ that there are different types of learning

KEY IDEAS
Learnacy
Learning to learn
Conscious and unconscious competence
The new 3Rs
The 5Rs
Tabula rasa
Experiential learning

5

Understanding Yourself as a Learner

The worst of all deceptions is the self-deception that we no longer need to learn.

after Plato

MOST OF US KNOW WHAT KIND OF BOOKS WE PREFER TO READ. SOME people love thrillers and hate science fiction, others prefer biographies or historical novels. The same applies to our eating habits. You may prefer Indian or Chinese food, vegetarian or organic, potatoes or rice, and so on.

But, what about your learning? To be a competent learner, you need to know a little more about the kind of learner you are. If you don't take the time to find out more, you may just be deceiving yourself into thinking that you cannot do something when in fact you can. What is special about you and the way you prefer to learn? And what can you do to work on those areas in you that are less developed?

There are three main factors determining your learning style:

1 Where you prefer to learn.
2 How you take in information most easily.
3 How you deal with information you have taken in.

You have already looked at the first of these in Chapter 3. Now, you need to think about how the other two affect your life.

Consider the following two examples.

Jennie has a strongly developed visual sense and she prefers to take in information in pictorial form. She loves using flipcharts or PowerPoint to visualize concepts and help her solve problems. She glazes over when colleagues at work give her densely written documents to comment on. She loves to think big and enjoys being creative and open-ended when dealing with new information. She is very much an afternoon person and loves group activities. She throws herself into projects and learns a lot from them, enjoys developing networks and doing voluntary work in the community. Jennie is very comfortable airing her opinions in meetings; indeed, she often uses such occasions to work out what she really thinks about an issue.

John cringes inwardly when his manager asks him to give his views to the rest of the team without any briefing beforehand. He is at his best in structured situations and hates ambiguity or uncertainty of any kind. He would much prefer to absorb information from an email that he can read on the train on his way into work. Like Jennie, John also enjoys solving problems, but his approach to dealing with information is quite different. He prefers to analyze the facts in a logical way, preferring systems and concepts. John loves to walk on his own, allowing a sensible order to settle on his sometimes worryingly contradictory thoughts. He is quiet and apparently withdrawn in many meetings and only comes alive on the squash or tennis court. He is reluctant to change unless the intellectual case has been made beyond doubt.

John is different from Jennie and both are different from you or me. Each one of us operates in different environments, takes in information differently, and deals with it in distinctive ways. Neither John nor Jennie is better than the other; indeed, each has useful skills for both business and home life.

Let's concentrate on how information gets to your brain in the first place.

HOW YOU TAKE IN INFORMATION

You take in information through your five senses that is fed into your brain. Four senses—hearing, some of sight, touch, and taste—

all go via the brain stem, your primitive brain. However, smell goes direct to the amygdala and into the olfactory nerves of your limbic system or mammalian brain. The sense of smell is, therefore, the quickest of your senses to register with you. (Perhaps our survival as a species has depended on our ability to discern meat that is "off" or the scents of our rivals!) Most people naturally favor one of their senses over the others.

Using your senses

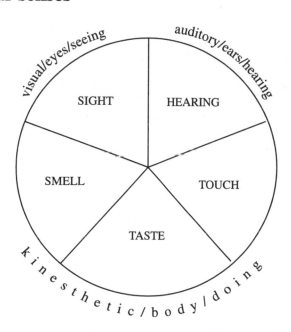

Think back over your day so far. Which of your senses have you used most? Which of your senses are the ones you rely on most? Is your answer the same for your home life as it is for work?

The three most common ways of receiving information are through your eyes, through your ears, or "through" your body. You see things, hear things, or get directly involved by experiencing them, often involving touch.

How do you best take in information? Using your eyes, your ears or your body?

- ❑ Do you tend to sit up straight in meetings and always try to look the speaker in the eye?
- ❑ Do you prefer reading than being read to, often snatching instructions from other people?
- ❑ Are you the kind of person who always remembers a face?
- ❑ Do you use maps rather than relying on verbal instructions?
- ❑ Do you take care to coordinate your appearance?
- ❑ Are you the first to get up and go to the flipchart and represent a problem as a diagram?

If you have answered yes to most of these questions, then you probably rely on your eyes most.

- ❑ Do you find yourself repeating the words being used by a presenter or nodding vigorously when someone is speaking to you?
- ❑ Perhaps you even stare into space and appear to be in a daydream, while you listen to your thoughts in your head?
- ❑ Do you like listening to music and to the radio?
- ❑ Are you the kind of person who always remembers a name?
- ❑ Are you happy to rely on verbal instructions?
- ❑ Do you tell jokes and enjoy a good debate when solving problems?
- ❑ Do you enjoy using the telephone?

If you have answered yes to most of these questions, then you probably rely on your ears most.

- ❑ Do you sometimes slump into your chair during meetings, frustrated that you cannot get up and walk around?
- ❑ Do you enjoy playing with your pen, with a rubber, with your personal organizer, or with your papers while someone is talking to you?
- ❑ Do you like outdoor pursuits?
- ❑ Do you tend to remember what happened rather than someone's name or even face?
- ❑ Are you expressive with your body?
- ❑ Are you the kind of person who wants to roll up your sleeves and do it rather than talking about it?
- ❑ Do you enjoy doing business while undertaking an activity at the same time?

If you have answered yes to most of these questions, then you probably rely on your body most.

Most people prefer one of these ways of taking in information. Some people, especially those who have consciously worked to develop different styles, may feel comfortable in two or three of them. In a typical group of people, about a third will naturally prefer to use their eyes, a third their ears, and a third their bodies. No one way is better than the others: they are simply different.

In most workplaces, information is shared using the written word or through verbal instructions. In meetings, as in most training rooms, people are not normally encouraged to get up and move around, when this is exactly what a sizable proportion of people would like to do.

A number of the leaders I interviewed are strongly visual. Hilary Cropper, chief executive of the FI Group, is a good example:

I like pictures. In management meetings I can't resist getting up to the flipchart. Drawing an idea gets a concept across much more clearly than numbers. You can express in images what you cannot yet put into words.

Chris Mellor, group managing director of Anglian Water, is similar: "I tend to visualize concepts, to think in metaphors."

Jayne-Anne Gadhia, managing director of Virgin One Account, talks in strongly visual terms. She remembers things visually, shunning all paperwork. And, when she is struggling with a difficult concept, she talks of "opening a door" in her mind to locate one of her role models to "ask" them what they would do in the situation.

When I meet senior executives, I am increasingly aware of how important and misunderstood this aspect of learning is. Many people simply glaze over when presented with the written word alone, but are instantly engaged if communication is by means of a diagram or chart.

How could you and your organization improve the range of its communication styles? What could you do to broaden your own range of communication styles and so increase their effectiveness?

The list overleaf contains many of the common ways in which information is shared in a company. Choose some techniques that you don't use and group them under the three headings of eyes, ears, and body to add to your repertoire.

- ✔ colorful flipcharts
- ✔ whiteboards
- ✔ post-it notes
- ✔ postcards
- ✔ short, personalized emails
- ✔ cartoons
- ✔ posters
- ✔ video
- ✔ newsletter

- ✔ intranet
- ✔ OHPs
- ✔ interactive display boards
- ✔ graffiti boards
- ✔ music
- ✔ role play/drama
- ✔ team briefings
- ✔ games
- ✔ word of mouth

The Centrica customer experience

When UK company Centrica wanted to communicate some key messages about customers to its staff, it chose an unusually imaginative way of engaging ears, eyes, and bodies with a learning maze.

Centrica has expanded rapidly from a company that owned British Gas to a broad-based services organization that includes a financial services arm, the Automobile Association (AA), breakdown recovery and insurance services, and various other ventures in the telecom and home security markets.

As these acquisitions and new ventures have taken place, the learning challenge was how to get 32,000 people to understand more about customers and opportunities, and then match their needs to the full range of products and services available—in short, to engage all the workforce by giving them the big picture, a story, and an interactive experience.

Purple Works, a specialist learning and communications company, designed a learning concept that relied on bringing together customer, product, and service information from all parts of the business and then presenting this in the form of a mobile, interactive exhibition.

The idea, which proved to be outstandingly successful, was to create an interactive multimedia learning experience in the form of an exhibition, a "learnibition." The creative team, led by Purple Works managing director Mark Watson, drew from the best of interactive museum display techniques, such as those adopted by London's Science Museum, and the most innovative practice in internal and external communication.

The design ensured that all learning styles were catered for and there was something for every employee, no matter how experienced or inexperienced. There were large visual panels for those who prefer to use their eyes. There were conversational activities aimed at those who like to listen. There were intriguing boxes fixed to the display that urged those who like to touch and experience things to open them. Employees were allowed to learn at their own pace and concentrate on the information that was relevant to them.

This approach enabled Centrica to learn about its customers and their changing needs in a fast, cost-effective way. It also allowed employees to connect with the bigger picture of Centrica as a new kind of business selling a range of products, mainly bought from the home, in addition to gas.

How could you organize more imaginative communication at work? Knowing what you now know about the need to give out information in a variety of modes, how might this affect the way you manage meetings? See pages 100–101 for more ideas about how to organize brain-friendly meetings.

DEALING WITH INFORMATION

How we deal with the information our senses bring us depends very much on the kind of personality we are. Our personality is a key determinant of the way we perceive information. At its simplest level, two people can see different things in the same picture.

This can be even more marked when words are involved.

So, if someone says to you, "That's a good idea!", you may hear either of the two alternatives below:

"That's a good idea! Great! A decision! I'm glad he likes it too. I'll go ahead and book the plane tickets."

"That's a good idea. So were the others we were considering. We've got to find out more before we decide whether to fly or take the train, or even hire a car and take the whole team."

It was Swiss psychiatrist Carl Jung who first described this area in detail. He divided people into feelers, thinkers, sensors, and intuitors. Jung's thinking has influenced many of the current tests used to describe individual personality styles. One of the most widely employed is the Myers-Briggs Type Indicator™. This seeks to uncover a person's natural preferences. There are 16 basic types, based around four main styles: intuitive thinkers, sensing thinkers, intuitive feelers, and sensing feelers. These four styles will tend to react in predictably different ways when they gather information and deal with the world. So, for example, sensing thinkers will prefer to rely on concrete facts, where intuitors will rely more on overall impressions. One of the advantages of the Myers-Briggs approach is that it is nonjudgmental and transfers well between home and work environments.

You have already seen this kind of approach when you learned about the two sides of the brain and the theories developed by Ned Hermann.

WORKING OUT YOUR LEARNING STYLE

British psychologists Peter Honey and Alan Mumford have developed a test that is widely used in organizations of all kinds. The test mainly focuses on the third of the three elements that go to make up an individual's learning style, how information is dealt with. It identifies four learning styles: activist, reflector, pragmatist, and theorist.

Without knowing any more, which word do you think best describes you as a learner?

Honey and Mumford's descriptions offer an accessible way of determining the way you prefer to put information you have absorbed into action. While they do not describe all the key elements of a learning style, they give a realistic and accessible view of your learning personality.

If you are an *activist*, you are the kind of person who is quick to roll up your sleeves and get stuck in. You enjoy the immediacy of experiences and are enthusiastic about anything new. You tend to act first and think later. You love being active and no sooner are you given a problem than you have begun to brainstorm solutions to it. You are probably gregarious by nature.

Your motto is: "I'll try anything once."

If you are a *reflector*, you tend to stand back from experiences, In meetings you probably take a back seat. You like to absorb a range of data before coming to any decision. You prefer to see the way things are going before offering an opinion of your own. You are probably cautious by nature.

Your motto is: "I'll need to think about that one."

If you are a *theorist*, you tend to think things through in a logical sequence until you can make it fit into a pattern. You like models, systems, and rules. You enjoy being detached and analytical. You can be a useful rigorous thinker and someone who will not budge from an opinion just because it does not fit your worldview.

Your motto is: "But how does it fit in with..."

If you are a *pragmatist*, you are always keen to try out ideas. You are always experimenting. You want to get on with things and not sit about talking. Once you have heard something interesting, you want to test it out straight away.

Your motto is: "There must be a better way."

Were you right in your first impressions of your learning style? Did you conclude, as many people do, that there were elements of two or three types in the way you operate? You can carry out a more detailed analysis of your preferred learning style by filling in a self-assessment questionnaire from Peter Honey Learning, see pages 258 and 259.

LEARNING STYLES AND INFORMATION PREFERENCES

It is possible to be a quiet activist and a noisy reflector. These categories do not allow you to denote the degree of emotional involvement you have as a learner. Neither do they distinguish between the absolutely key variations in the way you take in data: through your eyes and your ears and by using your body, which we explored earlier in this chapter. So, for example, you can be a theorist with a strongly developed preference for taking in information visually or auditorily.

To keep it simple, I suggest that a combination of two words, one from each of the following groups, will give you a more complete description of yourself as a learner.

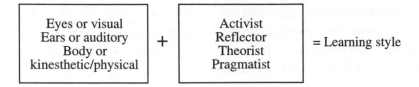

Eyes or visual
Ears or auditory
Body or
kinesthetic/physical   +   Activist
Reflector
Theorist
Pragmatist   = Learning style

Thus, there are 12 different possible combinations: visual/reflector, auditory/pragmatist, etc. Once you recognize these simple descriptions of different styles, work will never be the same again. You will suddenly be much better equipped to predict the ways in which your colleagues will react to certain situations and act accordingly.

When you are consciously aware of your preferred learning style, you can take steps to develop those areas that you do not instinctively prefer. You also become more aware of how and where you would ideally like to take in and process information. If you are facilitating a session or giving a presentation, you can make sure you don't stick rigidly to your own preferred learning style and run the risk of failing to hit most of your audience! If you are really interested, then you can also work out your Hermann Brain Dominance™ and Myers-Briggs™ profiles to give you additional information.

LEARNING STYLES AND MEETINGS

One moment where people's learning styles are particularly apparent is during meetings, as the two contrasting meetings in Annie's day in Chapter 1 made clear. Using the Honey and Mumford learning styles, you can see how the different types might react:

◆   Activists are the last to settle down at the start of a meeting. They want to brainstorm everything and are always reluctant to read any papers that have been tabled, preferring to talk about the practical issues being raised. When issues of long-term management are being discussed their eyes glaze over. They are often to be seen talking to their neighbor unless the meeting is being firmly chaired.

◆ Reflectors may often seem not to be fully engaged. They are reluctant ever to come to an agreement there and then, preferring to ask for time to think it through. They will enjoy tabling papers with new research or data to discuss. They find it difficult when urgent and unexpected decisions are needed at the meeting. They will tend to see new propositions from all angles and be reluctant to settle immediately on one course of action.

◆ Theorists can also be slow to settle. They are likely to be talking about structures and ideas that have interested them but may or may not be relevant to the meeting in hand. The theorists will want to challenge the basic assumptions underpinning any proposed course of action. They will not want to agree unless they can see how what is being proposed fits with their view of the world. Whenever anything is being considered that has a degree of risk, they will want to quantify the uncertainty. They are not comfortable with change until they have seen the new pattern within which it fits.

◆ Pragmatists are likely to be keen to get started. They do not worry when there is not an agenda, being happy to engage in whatever is offered for discussion. They have a tendency to be unpredictable and are likely to apply their latest theory or idea to whatever is being discussed. If they are stimulated by what is being discussed they will be engaged; if not they may be disruptive. They will be still be working on their ideas after it has been agreed what should be done and may well suggest revisions to things that others think have already been agreed.

Add to this what you know about the ways in which your colleagues prefer to take in information, and you will be well prepared.

Think about the best and worst meetings in which you have been involved. Put some people's names to the different Honey and Mumford types described above. In what other ways or situations are you aware of people's learning styles at work?

10 tips for holding brain-friendly meetings

If you want to get the best out of the minds around a table at any meeting in which you are involved, here are some more ideas:

1   *Always give advance notice of the subject of any meeting.* Your brain likes to make connections and to "join up the dots." Giving it something to think about in advance means that it will combine and link with existing thought patterns and knowledge to create new ideas.

2   *Make sure that meetings have a clear structure.* The brain likes to put things in order.

3   *Use praise.* Finding ways of praising people is likely to increase their self-esteem and create an environment in which people give their ideas. A praise to blame ratio of 4:1 is helpful.

4   *Invest time in creating the right emotional state in participants.* If your mind is stressed, it will only operate at the basic level it would need for survival. If we are not in a relaxed but alert state, then we will not perform well.

5   *Divide the content into smaller chunks.* Our brains work better when they can focus on specific elements. It may also be helpful to break things up into smaller elements to aid memory.

6   *Use humor.* When we laugh our brains release neurotransmitters, chemicals that boost alertness and recall.

7   *Use dialog.* Our brains thrive on feedback, of which dialog is a constant and immediate source. Telling someone something in a meeting does not mean that it has had any impact on their mind.

8   *Specify outcomes and connect to previous and following meetings.* The brain's love of connections and its ability to select what is relevant mean that it is a good idea to give it something to work on after the meeting. A mind map may be a better way of recording what happened than are traditional minutes.

9   *Watch people's concentration levels.* While we all have different concentration spans, having a stretch break regularly means that the brain gets plenty of oxygenated blood, its energy supply. Nevertheless, sometimes, when the brain is really engaged, it may be better to go with the flow.

10 *Spend time reflecting on what worked and what didn't.* Another important and often missing piece of feedback for the brain involves taking a few moments to talk about how a meeting went and plan to do things differently if it did not go well.

UNDERSTANDING YOURSELF AS A LEARNER—IN A NUTSHELL

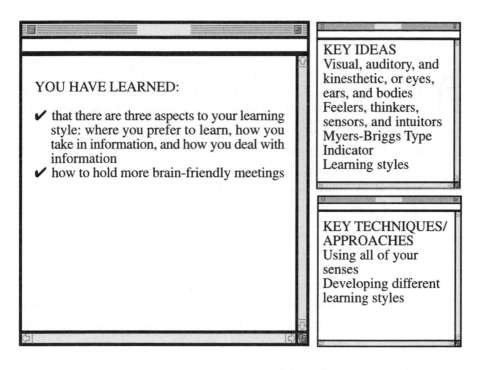

YOU HAVE LEARNED:

✔ that there are three aspects to your learning style: where you prefer to learn, how you take in information, and how you deal with information
✔ how to hold more brain-friendly meetings

KEY IDEAS
Visual, auditory, and kinesthetic, or eyes, ears, and bodies
Feelers, thinkers, sensors, and intuitors
Myers-Briggs Type Indicator
Learning styles

KEY TECHNIQUES/APPROACHES
Using all of your senses
Developing different learning styles

6

Resourcefulness

ALLOW ME TO TAKE YOU ON A SHORT FLIGHT OF FANCY. IMAGINE YOU ARE in a beautiful Scandinavian restaurant. You are wondering what to eat. Your waiter or waitress shows you a wonderful wooden platter of food, a *smörgåsbord*. On it are beautifully arranged portions of food. There are cold meats, fish, fruit, and vegetables, each laid out on different parts of the board. Luckily, you are in a restaurant frequented by tourists, and so each section of the platter is neatly labeled. You pick at will, sometimes pausing to read what it is you are eating, on other occasions simply savoring the delicious combination of tastes.

This is the image I want you to have of your own learning resources, the techniques that are at your disposal as a learner. You need to want to use them, just as you want to eat lovely food. You need, in short, to have an appetite for learning. If you explore the contents of the *smörgåsbord*, these are the kinds of phrases that appear on the labels:

Getting the big picture
Tuning in your mind
Using your memory
Chunking your learning
Learning by imitation
Learning online
Extending your range

In this chapter, I deal with some of the techniques you need to be a resourceful learner.

GETTING THE BIG PICTURE

We are surrounded by information. Data rushes past us in a fast-flowing torrent. We need some way of making sense of it.

Quite often, I go to meetings that start before anyone has the faintest notion of what the agenda is going to be. I sit and listen to speakers who fail to tell me, at the beginning of their speech, what they are going to talk about. I go to sessions where a trainer launches straight into things without any context. I work with companies undergoing major change programs where no one has made it clear to everyone concerned why they are happening, and everyone is circulating data that is apparently important and that few people actually understand. And, in my private life, I encounter many potentially enriching situations where information is being presented as if it were the only reality rather than a point of view.

This kind of experience is deeply frustrating for your brain. To be able to operate effectively, your brain likes, as you have already seen, to be able to make connections and see patterns between things. Deprive it of a context and it is much more difficult for it to connect what it is seeing or hearing or experiencing with what it already knows. It is also more likely that you will feel discomfort or anxiety as a result of trying to work out the relevance of what you are being faced with.

One of the most important learning to learn skills is the ability to ask questions that will enable you to check out the big picture. You may also need to interrupt the momentum of the situation to check out what is going on.

10 tips for asking for the big picture

1   I'm really sorry, but I don't know what this is about. Could you explain?
2   Have I missed something? This doesn't seem to fit with what I thought we were going to be doing. Perhaps you can explain.
3   Could you just go back over what it was you were planning to deal with in this session?

4   It would be really helpful if you could tell us what we are going to cover today.

5   It would help me if you could take a few moments to outline how you are going to be approaching this.

6   Exactly how does this fit into the overall picture?

7   Hang on! I really need you to stop and explain how this all fits into the bigger picture.

8   Could you possibly just take a little time to explain how this all fits into the bigger picture?

9   I really don't understand this. Please can you help me?

10   Could we all stop for a few minutes and agree an agenda for this session?

Think of some situations in your work or home life where you would have liked to have the big picture. Mentally rehearse some of the sentences above and adapt them to your own language and style.

People sometimes argue that they simply do not have time to stop and discuss what the best approach might be. They just present their approach as the only sensible one in the circumstances. This kind of attitude makes it less likely that the learning on offer will successfully engage the learners undertaking it.

Comments like the ones I have suggested may seem almost insultingly obvious to you. But, obvious or not, unless they are spoken early on in a learning episode, confusion and disconnection will reign.

As you grow more confident as a learner, you will work out other things that you may need to ask at the beginning of an activity. For example, you may want to find out more about:

◆   Your understanding of what is on offer: how long it will last, whether it is assessed, whether it is to be undertaken individually or in groups, how it fits in with other activities being planned.

◆   The purpose of what is on offer: whether it is seen as a social or an academic experience, what the objectives of the tutor or facilitator are.

◆   The media that will be used: how much will be interactive, how broad a range of learning methods will be used, whether some of the learning will be online.

It is quite possible to be put off learning something, even though you are really interested in the subject. In many cases it emerges, on further discussion, that you were turned off the very first time you attempted to do something, as my wife was from playing the piano.

As an adult learner (and as a child), by not asking questions like some of the ones we have been exploring, you can miss the critical moment of context when you could establish the connection between the learning being offered and your own life and needs. Perhaps if my wife had been able to ask questions that would have helped her understand what it was her music teacher wanted, she might have had a different experience when she was a child.

You may have felt a similar experience if you have ever been in a situation where you had something very difficult or sensitive to tell someone. Bad news is a good example of this. If you do not broach the subject immediately, all is lost. It becomes steadily more embarrassing to say what was on your mind.

If learning is to be successful, you need to connect to it actively. In the act of connecting you are, of course, creating opportunities for influencing the style of the learning. A facilitator who is asked to recap on what has gone before and what is planned for the session is being helped to do a better job. By asking questions about the use of different media, you are seeding ideas that may not otherwise have been in the mind of whoever is working with you. Of course, this needs to be done in such a way that it does not come over as one person "parading" their knowledge.

TUNING IN YOUR MIND

The process of connection is really about tuning in. Just as when you go abroad it takes a while for your ears to become attuned to the unaccustomed sounds of the strange language you hear, so it takes time for your mind to become attuned to the medium or method it is being invited to employ.

Your brain, as you have already discovered, loves patterns. You can put this characteristic to good use when it comes to tuning into learning.

Try these simple ideas before you start a particular learning activity:

◆ Cover a blank piece of writing or flipchart paper with all you already know about a subject. Take your time and keep on coming back to the task. Use a mixture of words, drawings, jottings—anything that seems helpful. I call this activity a braindrizzle. It is much less dependent on the accident of a particular time than a brainstorm and induces less unnecessary stress. By downloading what you already have in your mind, you are beginning to organize what you know.

◆ Set yourself some simple research tasks to do, like spending an hour on a focused web search or getting one good book from your library. Your mind is endlessly curious, so once you start to narrow the range you are beginning to tune in.

◆ Ask a member of your family, a friend, or a colleague to tell you what they know about the subject you are interested in. Other people tend to make connections that you have not considered.

◆ Browse and skim read as many books or magazines about your chosen topic and scribble anything interesting on to post-it notes. Put these up on a wall where you can see them. You can take in data at a very rapid speed. Surrounding yourself with visual prompts is a good way of engaging your brain.

◆ Make a list of all the questions you have about your area of interest. Your brain will naturally start to search out the connections/answers once it tunes in to this.

Simply by doing these kinds of activity, you are beginning to give your mind time to work on things before you start your learning. You will be amazed at its ability to process existing information and acquire new data so that you are well tuned in when you start out.

BREAKING DOWN YOUR LEARNING

It is important to set specific targets for your learning. To be a successful learner and achieve these targets, one of the key attributes you need is the ability to divide your learning into manageable, bite-sized chunks. "Breaking learning down into a series of hows" is how Peter Honey and I describe this skill.

This involves you in interrogating what it is you want to learn and breaking it down into appropriate chunks. Different aspects of it may then need different approaches. As the metaphor of interrogation suggests, you need to ask yourself some difficult questions. There are a number of techniques which may be helpful here.

Zooming in

This is an expression coined by Dr. Javier Bajer, chief executive of the Talent Foundation. It describes the process of putting learning under the microscope by progressively increasing the magnification so that you see more and more of what is involved in the learning. So, if you are thinking about learning to drive a car, you might start by seeing a car moving safely down the road with you as its driver. With a little more magnification, you might see a driving school and yourself sitting in a car being taught. Then, it might be a picture of your monthly diary showing your planned lessons and practice sessions. The next layer might show you in the car practicing reversing the car into a small parking space, and so on.

Naming the parts

Another technique, widely used in training, involves sticky labels. Get a large piece of paper of the kind that you have on a flipchart. Arm yourself with a pile of sticky labels. Think about the learning in which you are involved. Imagine your learning is a kind of machine and try and break it down into its constituent parts. Using the example of the car again, this could mean you writing down on your labels things like:

Learning to signal	Using the mirror
Learning to park	Understanding road signs
Overcoming my fear	Moving steadily

When you have done this, stick all the labels on to your paper and stand back. Now, see if you can group them together into helpful categories. Then work out what kind of approach you need to take with each group.

A useful prompt in this activity is to ask yourself questions beginning with who, what, where, why, when, and how.

Writing the recipe

You might like to see if you could describe your learning in terms of a recipe. For driving a car, your recipe could deal with the skills you need to learn to become competent, learning to start, changing gear, turning corners, etc. Or, it might be that you prefer to think of it consecutively in the way that a food recipe does:

Find a car
Find a driving school
Book a course of lessons
Arrange for practice sessions
Etc.

Whatever your chosen technique, with learning as with life, you need to be able to break down any task into achievable sections or chunks, to understand the series of "hows" you need to master.

LEARNING BY IMITATION

The saying "Imitation is the highest form of flattery" makes light of an enduringly contradictory aspect of human behavior. Stealing someone else's lines, unless you use quotation marks or clearly acknowledge them, is understandably considered to be a kind of theft. At school we are told not to cheat. For commercial ideas and products, copyright, patent, and trademark laws exist to provide a kind of protection. Yet, we know that smart people are those who can use other people's ideas for their own and others' benefit.

Given the competitive environment in which we find our-selves, it is not surprising that too many organizations have a culture discouraging all ideas that are NIH (not invented here). Somehow, ideas are seen as no good unless you thought of them first, a wholly brain-disregarding approach to learning!

In today's business environment, it is clearly commercial folly not to be continually on the lookout for good ideas. When these are found, they will often be imitated and copied.

Indeed, this is how your mind works. From your earliest days, when you were trying to copy the words you heard at home and then use them yourself, your brain has always been seeking to copy and imitate what it sees and hears. Then, as you grow up, you say things like "Show me how to do it, please," to ensure that you are given the chance to imitate a friend or family member, and, later on, a colleague at work.

It is important to make widespread use of this important facility of the brain's interest in imitation. This is a core tool of the Knowledge Age, where intellectual capital is the most important aspect of many organizations' value. Paradoxically, now that ideas have become the currency of success, it is even more important that we copy and learn from other people's. Whereas the theft of a thing leaves an obvious debt, the imitation of an idea simply breeds more ideas and leaves the original intact.

To be successful, you need consciously to seek to put yourself in as many situations as possible where you are likely to be able to imitate the best role models. This requires you to believe in the importance of this technique as a means of learning new things, recognize the social skills needed to enable you to copy others, and be prepared to move around to make it happen as a regular part of your learning life.

When Arie De Geus was launching Learning at Work Day for the Campaign for Learning at the headquarters of the British roadside assistance company the AA, he told a story, also related in his book *The Living Company*, which vividly illustrates the factors necessary for the skill of imitation to be effective in practice. At the start of the nineteenth century, milk was delivered to British homes in bottles without tops. Two of the country's best-loved songbirds, the robin and the blue tit, both rapidly learned how to drink the cream that gathered at the top of the bottle. In the 1930s, however, aluminum tops were placed on the bottles, sealing out both germs and songbirds.

By the 1950s, blue tits all over the UK had learned how to stick their beaks through the aluminum and drink the cream. But, to this day, robins have not managed to learn this. The reason, according to Berkeley professor Allan Wilson, is that robins are territorial birds, spending some of their time as breeding pairs, then much of the rest of it keeping rivals out of their areas. They have little or no chance to imitate each other. Blue tits, on the other hand, spend several months of each year in flocks of up to a dozen birds. As they move around from one garden to the next, they have the opportunity to imitate any bird that has learned the secret of the milk bottle top. Arie de Geus calls this behavior "flocking." It is an essential social ingredient of the idea of imitation. Of course, for this to work effectively, you have to be prepared to share knowledge as well as be intent on acquiring it!

Are you a robin or a blue tit in the way that you seek to imitate others? Are you happy for others to benefit from your ideas and experiences? What do you do to ensure that this happens effectively?

---

10 ways of ensuring you benefit from imitating others

1   *Spend time with the people you most admire in your organization.* In a very short time we pick up the mannerisms and approaches adopted by others close to us. It is important, therefore, to be discriminating in how you spend your time.

2   *Identify the people you most admire in your chosen line of work and find ways of watching them in action.* If you can imitate the best in your field you are likely to be more successful.

3   *Identify areas of your own performance that you would like to improve and think of the person in your organization who does those best.* This kind of specific imitation can be a very positive way of improving skills, for example, chairing a meeting or giving feedback.

4   *Seek out television programs or films that offer good examples to imitate.* Given your brain's tendency to imitate, be careful what you feed it.

5   *Read the biographies of people you admire.* Biographical writing often contains insights into successful behavior that can be imitated.

6   *Consciously spend time at lunch with the people you want to emulate at work.* Lunchtimes can often be wasted. If you can establish a social relationship with people you admire, you have more chance of discovering their success formulae.

7   *Consciously cultivate friends from different walks of life who exhibit behaviors you are seeking to model.* Often, it is when you are with people who do not share your assumptions that you can pick up useful insights.

8   *Avoid spending unnecessary time with people at work who are negative.* You will inevitably pick up some of their negativity.

9   *When you see a difficult situation being well handled, make a note of the ways in which this was done.* Be prepared to capture your own perceptions of what has worked well.

10   *Look out for social or learning opportunities at work where you may be able to extend your network of potential role models.* This is the way to be sure that you are "flocking with all kinds of birds."

Like many of the leaders I have interviewed, Colin Marshall, chairman of British Airways, sees a powerful leadership role here:

It is a leader's responsibility to share knowledge, expertise, and experience. Otherwise, the organization would lose its corporate memory and fail to grow. I share what I know through a formal process of review meetings and informally by day-to-day dialog and example. The result is a productive two-way flow because, as the man said, there's nothing so good for learning as teaching. One of the most important lessons to impart is the significance of internal communication to any business. In a company like British Airways, where much of the workforce is spread across the world at any one time, good regular communication is a vital management practice.

Increasingly, managers are working formally with a coach or mentor who will be able to be a critical friend to them, suggesting ways in which they can learn by imitation. In the list of skills that Peter Honey and I are developing, the ability to identify how much of your learning is solitary and how much is collaborative was considered to be the most important of all the skills of learning to learn.

Given the importance of the social dimension of imitation, the techniques outlined above would appear to be particularly important ones for you to acquire if you are to realize your potential.

LEARNING ONLINE

The second most important attribute that Peter Honey and I discovered was the ability to learn online. For most of us today, this is an inescapable element of our business lives. It is a subject where there is very little research into what works well and what does not.

In *The Future of Corporate Learning*, a survey for the UK's Department of Trade and Industry in 2000 that I co-wrote, we described the ways in which e-learning is becoming significant in almost all of the large organizations we looked at. Many of these had opted to create corporate universities, often largely virtual. Many are increasingly interested in how people actually learn. The British company BAE Systems is a good example of this. With over 100,000 employees across nine home markets throughout the world, it has not surprisingly decided to create a virtual university. It is significant that BAE has a faculty of learning alongside its international business school, its benchmarking and best practice center, and its more predictable engineering, research, and technology centers.

In 2000, the UK University for Industry (Ufi), the first government-backed e-university available to people of all educational backgrounds, was launched. Through a network of learning centers in businesses and community groups, Ufi seeks to make learning available in short courses online. And, of course, there are many corporate universities based in the US and elsewhere that have begun to offer electronic learning over the last decade.

To try to find out more about this aspect of learning to learn, the Campaign for Learning, management consultants KPMG, Ufi, and Peter Honey Learning recently collaborated on a survey of attitudes to e-learning.

Almost all of the people in our sample had participated in some kind of e-learning in the previous year. Their overall reactions toward e-learning were largely positive, with 90 percent feeling that it has been useful to them. These were the kinds of activities they undertook:

Involvement with e-learning in last 12 months	%
Surfed the internet for information	95
Updated knowledge by reading e-zines or electronic bulletins	64
Deliberately tried to develop new computer skills on your own, without being enrolled on a course	64
Been trained or helped in new computer skills on-the-job by a colleague or manager	36
Participated in email discussion group	33
None of these	3

Is this similar to your own patterns of behavior?

What tips do you have for effective surfing and searching?

What skills have you learned online?

How do you use email? Do you find email a positive or negative tool? How can you get others to use email in ways that are helpful to you?

How can you use discussion groups to help you learn?

While the majority of people are positive about e-learning, the words they associate with it are interesting:

Words best describing e-learning experienced	%
Convenient	56
Fast access to information	50
Working at my own pace	42
Impersonal	30
Frustrating	29
Lonely	16
Effective	14
Challenging	8
High quality	7
Tailored to my needs	7
Low quality	6
Stressful	5
Threatening	0
All positive comments	86
All negative comments	57

The data about how e-learning can be unhelpful gives a number of clues as to how you can learn more effectively online:

Ways e-learning can be unhelpful—Top 8	%
It's easy to waste time	46
Computer crashes	32
It's difficult to find relevant e-learning material	30
Learning programs or software are poor quality	26
Learning programs or software are too gimmicky	20
Learning programs or software are difficult to access	20
Takes up too much time	17
Impossible to learn without other people	11

Does this data accord with your own experience of online learning?
What does the data in the chart above suggest to you about ways in which you could improve your own online learning?
How much e-learning are you already doing?
There are many new e-learning providers: have you considered trying some?

EXTENDING YOUR RANGE

To be an effective learner you need to be prepared to try new things and always be trying to extend your range. This is specifically stated in the skills that Peter Honey and I identified: "Constantly adding new techniques to your repertoire from all possible sources" and "experimenting, on a trial-and-error basis, with different ways of learning."

The truth is that we all have our learning comfort zones and that most of us move out of these too rarely. Taking part in an action learning set—exploring real business issues in a team—or being mentored may be within the existing range of one person, but they may be new to somebody else. Only you will know what is new for you!

This is as true for those at the bottom of organizations as it is at the top, as the following example shows.

The Campaign for Learning hosted a breakfast meeting for chief executives of large companies. Our purpose was to interest them in the issue of learning. Our main way of doing this was through the inspirational speaking of Charles Handy, who kindly gave his time to help us do this.

We could have simply enjoyed what a man of his insights wanted to say, had some conversations over our coffee, and then gone our separate ways. I am sure that this would have been a wonderful experience for all present.

But, at the time of the breakfast Charles and his wife Elizabeth had just published *The New Alchemists*, their compelling examination, in words and photographs, of some extraordinary individuals living in London. In most of these portraits there were strong connections to be made between personal events in the past and their views about learning and its value to their business today.

Working with a specialist learning and communications company, Purple Works, we created some learning mats, based on ideas contained in *The New Alchemists*. The mats were designed, in full color, to provide visual stimulus to conversations over breakfast, focusing on areas such as the influence of school, family, trauma, failure, and the context of a very rapidly changing world. They were placed on the tables as highly unusual tablecloths.

From many of the chief executives who attended, you could sense an immediate "What's all this then?" sort of reaction. Learning mats were not in their current learning comfort zones. But, inspired by Charles Handy, all of those present rapidly overcame any initial apprehensions and discovered just how useful such a tool could be in structuring conversation without the need for intrusive facilitation.

The chief executive of a large construction company told me afterwards that he had not been so stimulated for years and volunteered quite personal information about a traumatic sporting experience that had powerfully shaped his personality at work. He had clearly enjoyed journeying outside his comfort zone.

Where does your own learning comfort zone stop? Look through this book, especially the A–Z of techniques at the back. How many of these have you not tried? Choose one new one to focus on over the coming month.

As Tom Peters puts it:

The good news—and it is largely good news—is that everyone has a chance to learn, improve, and build up their skills.

RESOURCEFULNESS—IN A NUTSHELL

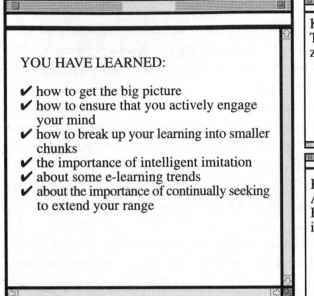

YOU HAVE LEARNED:

✔ how to get the big picture
✔ how to ensure that you actively engage your mind
✔ how to break up your learning into smaller chunks
✔ the importance of intelligent imitation
✔ about some e-learning trends
✔ about the importance of continually seeking to extend your range

KEY IDEA
The learning comfort zone

KEY TECHNIQUE/ APPROACH
Breaking learning down into its component parts

7
Remembering

T HE RELATIONSHIP BETWEEN MEMORY AND LEARNING IS CLEARLY A VERY
important one. It is also an area where there has been a certain
amount of misleading writing, especially in the popular press. So,
you can read about foods that are meant to improve your memory
dramatically and techniques that are claimed to transform your life
for ever. The danger is that the hype gets in the way of the kind of
basic understanding that undoubtedly *will* help you to improve
your memory.

An interesting question is the degree to which, as Dr. Pierce
Howard puts it, "learning is memory that sticks." Is learning the
sum of all the things we remember? Or, do we remember some
things that are only really learning in the sense that all experience
is learning?

Much of our learning is retained at a subconscious level. It
exists at the level of tacit knowledge, which is extremely important
to have and which is often very difficult to explain or describe. It
may have stuck, but recalling it is instinctive rather than conscious.
Think back to the description in Chapter 4 of how we move from
unconscious incompetence to unconscious competence in many of
the key areas of our learning.

Unfortunately, many people associate memory negatively
with school or professional examinations. It was something you
needed so you were able to pass tests. It is powerfully linked in your
mind to stressful times.

For most of us, there are very real reasons for an effective
memory being important. Without one, we arrive at work lacking
the things we need. We leave meetings without catching the person

we need to speak to. We forget key details of a person's face and feel foolish when we cannot remember them. This kind of need is the subject of small advertisements in the mainstream press. There is a belief somehow that you can acquire a miracle cure or treatment to improve your memory.

From time to time interesting articles appear about what is going on in the brain. Recently, for example, most of the British serious and tabloid press covered the story of how the hippocampus area of the brain was more developed in London taxi drivers than in most "ordinary" people. The hippocampus is where certain kinds of memories are stored and it seems that London taxi drivers, famous for having "the knowledge"—the names of streets and the routes to and from anywhere in the city to any other place—had made so many neural connections in this particular area of their brain that it had expanded accordingly.

However, harnessing knowledge is not just an issue for taxi drivers: we all need to be able to do it. Managing knowledge effectively, in business and in your personal life, depends on having at least a basic understanding of how your memory works and what you can do to avoid being the kind of person for whom things are always "on the tip of their tongue."

UNDERSTANDING HOW YOUR MEMORY WORKS

Before you attempt to grapple with the science of memory, it is important to remind yourself that there are two different elements of what most of us think of as memory:

1   Fixing the memory in the first place.
2   Recalling the memory when you need it.

What is actually going on in your mind when you are using your memory is, not surprisingly, extremely complex. Rather than focusing on any one single area, scientists increasingly think that a number of different ones are involved, often almost simultaneously, depending on the particular kind of experience. It seems likely that various parts of your learning brain—the cortex area, the amgydala, and the hippocampus especially—all have roles to play.

Every time you sense something, an electrochemical connection is made. It leaves a trace or pathway of connections between your synapses. Each one of these is, potentially, a memory. The more a particular pattern of connections is activated, the more likely it is that a memory will be created. For the memory to stick, however, it has to mean something: your brain has to find some meaning in it. Relevance to something you are already interested in may help a memory to stick. Emotions also play an important part. Chemicals are produced that act as effective transmitters to help you lay down effective memories. It seems likely that, in moderate amounts, the two neurotransmitters adrenaline and noradrenaline (also known as epinephrine and norepinephrine) act as fixers, helping to ensure that a memory becomes long term. (You probably remember where you were and who you were with when you had your first kiss, for example!)

However, if the emotion is so intense that your survival is threatened, then your adrenal glands start to work more energetically, in case you need to fight it out or run away. If the stress continues, you may start to produce another chemical called cortisol, which decreases your effectiveness to learn or remember.

To understand your memory, it may be helpful to have a much clearer idea of how many different activities are encompassed by this extraordinary capability. I started this section by distinguishing between laying down a memory and recalling it when needed, but there are many other ways of looking at memory that may also help you to be clearer about what you mean.

TYPES OF MEMORY

Explicit or implicit?

You remember how to walk, talk, kick a football, drive a car, or ride a bicycle implicitly. In other words, you do not have to consciously remember what to do. In contrast, you have to be explicit about remembering how to use the keys to someone else's front door if you have only been shown once. Or, when you see someone whose face you definitely know but cannot immediately place, you have to work out where you last saw them and find some way of triggering your memory of their name.

Instant, short term, or long term?

The fact that you do not remember everything you experience is part of your brain's survival mechanism. You mostly remember what you need to, what is important to you for some reason. In a typical day there are many items that are only ever going to be part of your instant memories lasting a few seconds only—for example, what cereal you have eaten, the color of the pen you have just picked up, or the number plate of the car in front of you. Then there are short-term memories—what you need to take to work, who is picking up your children, where you are going.

Luckily for you, much of the trivia of life—who said what to whom—is almost instantly forgotten. But, the important things need to be kept for the longer term. You learn and remember how to cross a road safely, for example, by learning and recalling the noise and sights that indicate the presence of cars. You store memories of what a particular gesture or tone of voice conveys and consequently know when someone is getting angry or upset.

Some of your instant, short-term, and long-term memories are implicit, some are explicit.

Is memory about items of information or processes?

Your memory clearly has to deal with individual items: the image of your own house, a particular face, a word, or a symbol. But it also has to store memories of important processes, like some of the examples we have already suggested: driving a car, kicking a ball, or putting a key in a lock.

KEY MEMORY PRINCIPLES

So, what does all this mean for you in your life at work and at home? When it comes to how your memory works, there are a number of simple principles to understand.

1 You tend to remember the first and the last items. This is sometimes called the primacy and recency effect.
2 If you can find the patterns and connections between items, this will help you to remember them.
3 You tend to remember things that are surprising or odd, that do not conform to patterns.
4 Your ability to recall things is improved if you review what you have learned over a period of time.

Each of these principles has a direct impact on your life. In the workplace, for example, the following apply:

Principle	Activity	Implications
You tend to remember the first and the last	Meetings	Break meetings up into a number of mini-meetings to create more beginnings and endings. Make sure the items with which you start and end a meeting are the ones you want people to remember. Don't necessarily leave the item that will be most con-troversial until last, as it may leave people with unneces-sary negative feelings. Take regular short "stretch" breaks.
	Communications	In one-to-one discussions, make sure that the first and last things you say are strongly positive.
	Making presentations	Concentrate on starting and ending strongly!
	Learning	Take regular breaks, splitting your learning up into chunks.

Principle	Activity	Implications
If you can find the patterns and connections between items, it helps you to remember them	Meetings	Help people to make connections between apparently unconnected items where this would be helpful, for example, if you are discussing something routinely on business agendas such as cost cutting, by making a connection using humor, a strong image, or an acronym.
	Learning	As above. See also the specific techniques on page 100.
You tend to remember things that are surprising or odd, that do not conform to patterns	Internal communications	Advertisers have long known that we remember the incongruous, but those responsible for communicating with staff inside organizations have been slower to realize this. Use surprising images to reinforce routine but important messages, for example, about health and safety.
	Making presentations	Seek out examples from outside your field of work or specialist interest. Your audience may remember the surprising patterns they create.
	Learning	Actively seek to make connections between things you have learned. For example, before the end of a training course, make up a simple rhyme with all the key learning points you want to recall.
Your ability to recall things is improved if you review what you have learned over a period of time	Meetings	As you go through meetings, repeatedly make interim summaries of what you have agreed and where you are going. Always start a meeting by recapping what you agreed last time.
	Internal communications	Refer to and build on previous campaigns. Use the intranet to send repeat and reminder messages to staff.
	Learning	Review what you have learned regularly. See also the specific techniques on pages 130–31.

The individual who has done more than anyone to promote an understanding of how your memory works is British expert Tony Buzan. In books like the bestselling *Use Your Head*, Buzan provides many practical activities to help you develop your memory. He has also invented a way of visualizing thoughts, the mind map™.

To make a mind map, turn a piece of paper through 90 degrees so that its shortest side is vertical. Put the title of your map or a picture in the center and draw an oblong around it. Pick out the main topics or headings of whatever you are mapping. Draw lines out from your central oblong toward the edge of the page and label the line as you do it. Then draw smaller lines, like branches of the trunk of a tree, from each of your main lines. You can also create twigs off the branches if you think of something else that is part of a branch. Once the basic shape of the map is taking place, you can add connecting lines to link different branches. You can also annotate the map with colors, question marks, underlining—anything that helps you make connections.

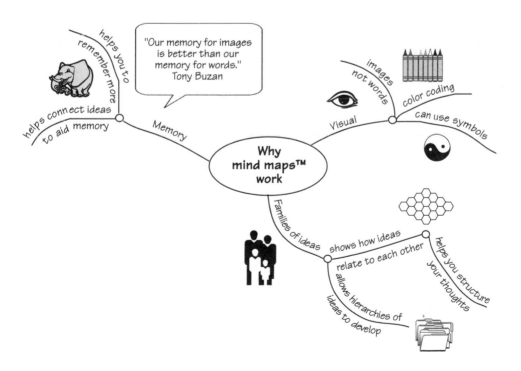

You will have noticed that each of the three parts of this book starts with a mind map. Such maps are a very helpful way of showing visually what you are about to read. I also find that they are useful as a method of capturing my thoughts when I am writing an article or preparing a speech.

If you are not familiar with this style of note making, make a mind map of the things you want to do this coming weekend and see how it works for you.

An excellent example of someone who really uses her visual memory is Jayne-Anne Gadhia, managing director of the UK financial services company, Virgin One Account. Jayne-Anne never writes things down. Instead, she "visualizes lists." As a busy executive, she always has a million and one things going on. Yet, she very rarely forgets anything and can surprise her secretary with her total recall of detail. To ensure that she can focus on one thing at a time, she has developed an interesting technique, managing her memory through visualization:

I think of my mind as a set of new pigeonholes. At any one time I only ever have one open. I consciously visualize the closing and opening of the pigeonholes.

Colin Marshall also has strong views about this area:

I believe everyone has a latent photographic memory. It simply has to be exercised and trained in order to achieve its potential for organizing and remembering things. I have no mnemonics that I am conscious of, but find that if I concentrate on statistics and information, making a mental picture of the words and numbers, they stay with me.

Another interesting approach to note taking is called "free-noting." It was invented by American Win Wenger and is the note-taking equivalent of brainstorming. Instead of organizing your notes into a map or a series of linear notes of the kind that many of us were taught at school, you write down whatever comes into your head during a learning experience. Instead of trying to group your thoughts, you simply allow your pen (or fingers if you are using a laptop computer) to wander as you listen or watch.

The theory behind this kind of approach is that it allows ideas to enter your mind more freely and subliminally as well as consciously. It also makes it more likely that you will connect the learning to your more personal thoughts and so be likely to remember it more clearly.

> *Put this book down for a second and try some free-noting. Write down whatever comes into your head from reading this book so far.*

Whichever style of note taking you choose to adopt, it is important that you make the notes yourself, as this is a key element of the engagement process.

Other useful techniques include:

◆   Using highlighter pens to focus on the things you want to remember.
◆   Creating patterns or charts to capture relationships between items.
◆   Using sticky notes to break up complex information into smaller chunks.

In the context of the workplace, there are some very simple ways of helping everyone to remember more by creating a number of templates for employees to use. These could include:

1   *Preprinted sheets* for internal and external meetings and for team briefing sessions that do not simply allow space for action points, but also have areas for mind mapping and free-noting.
2   *Proformas for all training sessions* with checklists of various prompt questions, for example: Have you asked for or been given the big picture? Do you know the "who, why, what, how, where, and when" of what you are going to learn? You could also add statements like: The three best ideas from the session were... The key thing I want to remember is...
3   *Graffiti boards* in public areas where people can write down their good ideas.
4   *Posters with sayings and quotations* supportive of the kinds of things

you have been learning and ideally generated by employees, as well as using sayings from well-known people.

5   *Large flowcharts for new projects or change management programs*, and encouraging employees to add their comments using sticky labels, Blu-tac™, or magnetic strips.

There is a well-known group of sayings that apply some of these principles about memory in an instantly useful way:

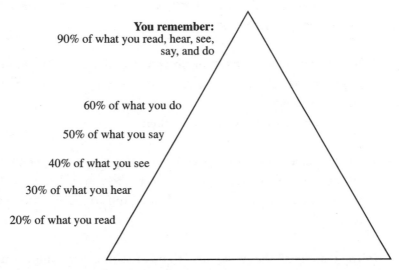

You remember:
90% of what you read, hear, see, say, and do

60% of what you do

50% of what you say

40% of what you see

30% of what you hear

20% of what you read

Of course, the percentages may only be roughly right. And as you get higher up the scale, you are really describing experiential learning in which you are fully involved. Nevertheless, they are strongly indicative of an important trend.

What implications does this information have for you at work? How often do you create opportunities for those you work with to engage their senses when learning?

MEMORY PEGS

You have already seen, in the chart on pages 121–2, a few of the ways in which the four key principles of memory can affect your life at work. In this section we will look in a little more detail at how you can apply these and other principles.

An underlying idea of all four memory principles is that to retain things, you need to connect with them to ensure that they stick in the memory. Another way of looking at this is to think of your brain as if it were your garden, with a rather unusual clothes line to which various items have been pegged. This line is strange because the things that are attached to it are not your clothes, but all the bits and pieces you want to remember. So, there are lists, bills, photographs, and jottings pegged to it.

A common way of "pegging" a sequence of words or ideas so that you will remember them is an acronym, or word constructed out of the first letters of various other words. Joyce Taylor, managing director of Discovery Networks Europe, has developed one— SPIRIT—with her staff to sum up their corporate values:

Simple
Passionate
Inspiring
Refreshing
Involving
Trustworthy

The acronym is used regularly by Taylor and her staff and she has written it in the personal work book she carries around with her. It is useful because each of the words has a clear meaning and together they serve as a regular useful reminder of the sort of business that Discovery wants to be.

Acronyms work best when they act as a peg for key elements of a belief system or, as British accelerated learning expert Colin Rose has shown, when they help you to remember the ordering of an important process. Rose applies the acronym MASTER to the process of how to learn:

Mind relaxed
Acquire the facts
Search out the meaning
Trigger the memory
Exhibit what you know
Reflect on the process

At a very practical level, the reason acronyms may be important to us is that we can only carry a limited number of items of information in our heads, unless we can write them down. Interestingly, in some oral cultures there are no words for large numbers. In Australia, it seems that the original aboriginal inhabitants of the island only have words for the first six numbers. After that, there is just one word for a number that is greater then six. Maybe our minds are not naturally geared up to remembering more than seven or so new bits of information—which perhaps accounts for the prevalence of business books with "seven" in their titles or chapter headings.

Do you use acronyms at work or at home? Are there important processes that you would remember more effectively if you created an acronym for them?

THE IMPORTANCE OF WHERE YOU ARE

Place is also a powerful way of anchoring memories. For example, many people can remember exactly where they were when important personal, world, or sporting events took place. This may be because of the emotions such events create, or because the events are so extraordinary that they are surprising or odd when set against the normal pattern of things, like walking on the moon or a terrible disaster of some kind. This effect can be put to good use.

You can consciously seek to absorb the details of a place as you experience something that you are determined to remember. I find that this works well for me when I am in a meeting and want to remember something in particular. In addition to my notes or a mind map, I consciously connect the memory to the place I am in, looking carefully around the room, so that I can recall the thought later on. In these examples, it is likely that place is providing an extra context to which your mind can "connect" a particular thought. Some of the places also may act as emotional triggers.

Have you had experiences like this?

These examples point to another feature of memory, the way it can engage all of your senses. I can still, for example, remember the strong smell of the polish on the floor of my first school; with the remembered smell, a flood of childhood memories comes back to me. Memory is multilayered and often works like this.

Do you have memories that are triggered for you by sensory input?

MUTTERING

Many people find it helpful to fix processes in their mind by muttering—speaking about their constituent elements out loud as they go through them. While this may seem a strange thing to do at work, don't worry! It's not as crazy as it seems at first and it gets results.

A good example of how this can operate is when you need to learn a new computer skill. Think for a moment of how often you ask someone to help you do something new. You do it once while they are there, anxious to get on with the task in hand and only half listening to what they are saying. Then they go back to their work and you are left on your own, It is a sure bet that, as soon as they have gone, you find that you can't remember how to do the new task. Next time this happens, say that you would like to talk the task through as you do it to help fix it in your memory: "I've opened my email. Now I am looking for x under the y menu. Now I am going to check on z, etc." By muttering as you do something, you are continually reflecting on what you are doing, analyzing it, applying it, asking questions about it. This undoubtedly helps you develop a vocabulary to describe and then fix your learning in your mind.

There are two logical extensions of muttering: creative visualization and teaching.

Creative visualization enables you to anticipate new experiences by rehearsing them. This is widely used by athletes and theatrical performers. You close your eyes and imagine yourself going through the experience, mentally talking yourself through each stage. I find this especially helpful before:

- ◆ difficult meetings, when I rehearse different answers to possible reactions
- ◆ speeches or presentations, when I concentrate on the first few minutes of my talk and picture the audience in front of me, imagining different possible reactions
- ◆ any written assignment, when I imagine the story of my argument and then often scribble it down as a flowchart or mind map.

The second approach involves taking the idea of talking yourself through the experience one stage further. You put your memory to the test by teaching what you have learned to someone else. Anyone who has tried to do this knows that it is a very effective measure of how much you have retained yourself. Not only is this a good method of reinforcing your memory, it also sends out very positive signals about you as a manager and coach, taking time to value and share what you have learned. Obviously, this idea extends way beyond learning new computer skills.

MAKING REGULAR DEPOSITS IN YOUR MEMORY BANK

Whether you remember something depends not only on the power of the initial experience, but also on how you review what you have learned. A good rule of thumb is to try to remind yourself of important things that you want to remember:

an hour later
a day later
a week later
a month later
three months later.

It may be that you only spend five or ten minutes reviewing what you learned, perhaps using your notes or some kind of visual aid to help you. But, if you do this you will be able to improve your recall by at least a factor of four.

It is helpful to think of your memory as a bank that has lent you money for a significant purchase like a house or a car and requires regular savings or deposits for you to be able to realize your investment. Regular reinforcement over a period of time has been shown greatly to increase the capacity to recall things.

By the same token, research has shown that you tend to remember things in proportion to the amount of time you have spent learning them, and that, if possible, you should try to spread out your learning over a number of regular episodes rather than taking it in one concentrated experience. This is not to say that in-depth experiences are not valuable or memorable. Indeed, they often are precisely so because of the emotional engagement they demand of their participants. Nevertheless, it is important, in these kinds of situations, that what was learned is regularly reviewed.

You may recognize this from your own experience of reading a good book on holiday. Often, a vacation gives you the opportunity to read a book right through in a few days. But, how much of it can you remember a few weeks later? Not very much is retained unless you have found some way of keeping the experiences alive in your mind for longer, allowing the patterns of neural connections to become a little more established. Some adults can still remember the details of texts they studied as a young student precisely because their study was spread over a significant period and regularly reviewed.

YOUR SLEEPING MIND

In science fiction you sometimes read scenes where the villain attempts to "brainwash" the hero by programming him with audio-tapes played while he is asleep. The belief, a mistaken one, was that you could somehow force the brain to remember things if it was played them while asleep.

This is clearly not possible, but there is no doubt that very mysterious things go on while we are asleep. Our brains, released from absorbing data during their waking hours, seem to have time to process and make sense of it. We even say things like "I'll sleep on it" in the hope that inspiration will come to us. And it often does. Indeed, many of the world's most famous inventors and

artists cite revelations that have come to them in dreams or immediately on waking from sleep.

Researchers have discovered that your memory does not
function as well if you do not get enough sleep. Some have suggested that the deep sleep called REM (rapid eye movement) sleep
is critical in enabling the brain to make sense of what has happened
during the day. (See pages 26–8 for more information on the brain
and sleep.)

Jayne-Anne Gadhia puts it like this:

*I began to realize that if I went to bed worrying about something I would
often have found the answer when I woke up. So now I deliberately pop a
question into my mind before I go to sleep. In the morning when I am having a shower I consciously ask myself for the answer and almost invariably it
comes into my mind. I now use this technique as a means of solving problems.*

Sir Bob Reid, deputy chairman of the Bank of Scotland and someone with a wide experience of leading large companies, finds that
sleep works in a different way for him:

*I dream a lot. In the midst of intense periods of work my dreams are always
happier. When I am more relaxed or in the middle of intense physical activity, I tend to have less happy dreams.*

I have a simple way of dealing with the thoughts that I often have
in the middle of the night. Like many people, I find that good ideas
or things I want to remember pop into my head just at the moment
when I want to be sleeping. To make sure that I capture my ideas
and at the same time minimize the interruption to my rest, I keep
a few items by my bed—a magazine, a book, a spare pillow—which
I gently throw toward my bedroom door (ensuring that I will have
to walk over them when I get up in the morning). I hardly need to
stir as I do this. As I turn over to go back to sleep, I actively associate the item I have thrown with the thought I have had and "tell"
my brain to remember it in the morning when I get up.

Bizarre as this may sound, it works well for me. In the morning I see, or trip over, the item and recall the thought I had earlier

in the night. I also keep a pencil and notepad by my bed in case my thought is too complex to be fixed by my strange nocturnal throwing game and needs to be written down!

Knowing what you now do about how your memory functions, think of at least three things that you could do differently at work to help people recall more. Don't be afraid to use highlighter pens on the pages you have been reading or to make notes in the margins!

In so many way it is true to say that, as Accelerated Learning expert Colin Rose puts it: "There can be no learning without memory."

REMEMBERING—IN A NUTSHELL

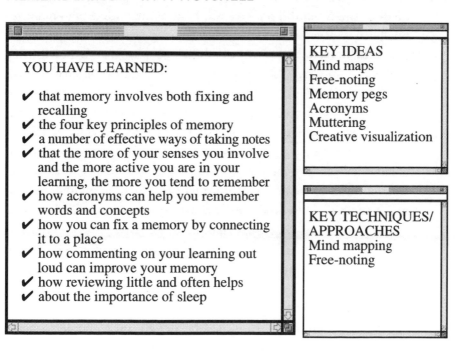

YOU HAVE LEARNED:

✔ that memory involves both fixing and recalling
✔ the four key principles of memory
✔ a number of effective ways of taking notes
✔ that the more of your senses you involve and the more active you are in your learning, the more you tend to remember
✔ how acronyms can help you remember words and concepts
✔ how you can fix a memory by connecting it to a place
✔ how commenting on your learning out loud can improve your memory
✔ how reviewing little and often helps
✔ about the importance of sleep

KEY IDEAS
Mind maps
Free-noting
Memory pegs
Acronyms
Muttering
Creative visualization

KEY TECHNIQUES/ APPROACHES
Mind mapping
Free-noting

8

Resilience

L OOK AT A YOUNG CHILD TRYING TO WALK OR DESPERATELY SEEKING THE right word to convey their thoughts. Imagine all the great inventors of the world and all the stories about how they tried and failed hundreds of times but did not give up. Picture the athlete who manages finally to trim a few seconds off a personal best time by persisting with their technique. All of these people are demonstrating resilience. As Guy Claxton puts it: "Without the ability to take good decisions about what, when, where and why to learn, and to tolerate the emotional concomitants of learning, especially when it gets difficult, learning power has no foundation on which to build."

Hilary Cropper, chief executive of the FI Group, is adamant about the business value of this attribute: "Resilience is essential. But you need to create an environment in which individuals are not under too much stress. People can live with ambiguity if they have a base from which they can expand."

Resilience is a key element of individual and species evolution. If you are resilient, you are more likely to survive and thrive. For many people, home, school, college, and workplace have done them no favors with respect to this attribute.

First, there is an emotional barrier in most people to being open when things get tough, so we don't show the sweat on our brow or the pain in our heart because it looks like an admission of failure, or because we have been humiliated if we did this in the past.

Secondly, the culture of too many learning environments—both informal, like the family, and formal, such as school—is to give up when the going gets tough. So, if a child has a tantrum, instead of helping them to work through it, parents allow it to continue unchecked. You can see this behavior happening all the time with children in the supermarket. Any adult who has tried to get fit in a gym or learn a musical instrument they have never played before knows that if you gave up after the first bead of perspiration appeared on your brow, you would never get anywhere. Or, it may be that you, your child, or, indeed, your boss, has developed skillful techniques for evading the discomfort associated with learning, from tantrums to sulking. These are displacement activities that allow you to pretend that something else is more important than being resilient.

Thirdly, we don't teach resilience in schools or, for that matter, at work, because we put too much emphasis on knowledge, not enough on certain skills, and almost nothing on key attitudes such as resilience. We fail to learn how to be resilient. When children learn to walk, they tend to progress naturally from crawling to walking by holding on to items of furniture and then reaching for parental hands. In so doing, they learn a certain amount of resilience. But if you give a child a "baby walker," they can easily become overdependent on it, only walking in a limited sense of the word. It is similar for learning.

The reward systems of many organizations do not value resilience. Consequently, they engender a culture of short-term thinking and discourage employees from seeing things through.

The kinds of techniques required to be resilient include:

- Persisting with new learning methods until they become easier.
- Pondering the different feelings, pleasant and unpleasant, triggered by different learning experiences.
- Deliberately choosing challenging learning options.
- Experimenting on a trial-and-error basis with different ways of learning.
- Pondering your original motives for learning and the ones that keep you going.
- Getting in touch with the feelings and emotions that suffuse learning.
- Answering the question: "How can I improve the way I learn?"
- Accepting accidental, unplanned experiences and working out how they contribute to your learning.
- Undertaking activities to strengthen learning skills and/or overcome weaknesses.

How resilient are you? Use the chart below to help you review your own skills, based on the list above.

Resilience activity	How good are you?
Persisting	
Pondering	
Choosing challenging learning options	
Experimenting	
Staying motivated	
Being in touch with feelings	
Knowing how you can improve	
Accepting unplanned experiences	
Overcoming weaknesses	

There are four main areas of resilience to work on: how you persist, being an adventurer, dealing with difficulties, and dealing with confusion.

PERSISTENCE

To make any progress with anything, learning to learn included, you need to persist with new learning methods until they become easier. You have to keep going when other conflicting pressures crowd in on you. At the simplest of levels, you need to learn how to concentrate. You have already seen how the brain likes to have regular short breaks. And later in this section you can discover what is happening when you are in a state of flow and time has almost lost any meaning for you. The truth is that we all have different concentration spans.

At a practical level, there are simple things you can do to improve your persistence. The list below gives you some ideas.

1   Set a clear objective for the session and try not to stop until you have achieved it. But, be prepared to stop if you discover something you had not anticipated and rethink your objective.

2   Make sure that you leave a message on your mobile phone and email that lets people know that you will not be replying to them for the duration of your learning. Turn off all telephones.

3   Make sure that there are no distracting noises around you.

4   If you start to daydream, get up and walk around.

5   If you are hungry, have a sensible snack and drink some water.

6   Have a list of all your normal displacement activities—making a cup of coffee, turning on a TV or radio, doing things that are easy, irrelevant, and not urgent—and ration yourself very carefully over the way you indulge in them!

7   Tell your colleagues, friends, and family that if you try to get them to divert you from your chosen learning activity, they are to tell you to "get on with it" and to go back to concentrating on the task in hand.

Focusing on developing your preferred learning style is one way of playing to your strengths and may make it easier for you to persist. In Chapter 3 you also looked at rewards and how these can be used to help you keep going, and in Chapter 1 you saw the effect of food and drink on your ability to concentrate.

> *Think of something you are currently trying to learn but finding it difficult to keep going with. Apply some of the ideas above to that activity.*

BEING AN ADVENTURER

We all started out as adventurers when we were young children, but somehow we seem to lose this important characteristic.

You have already seen how the brain is continually trying to search out information and make sense of it. You have also seen how it likes to form patterns and make connections. The most successful learners use the patterning tendency of their mind but do not get too set in the ways they think about things. (There is more about this creative aspect of learning later in this section.) They are always searching, inquiring, and wanting to find out more. They are adventurers who don't mind challenging accepted ways of doing things, are open to being spontaneous, and are prepared to take calculated risks. As you will recall from the section on learning and personality types in Chapter 4, each person will, of course, express their adventurousness differently.

Hilary Cropper is a good example of someone who does not like formal learning but clearly has a spirit of adventure. Indeed, at the FI Group she has made a name for herself as someone who advocates joint ventures as a way of trading. She says of herself:

I hate being taught anything. But I love being put into situations where I don't know what to do and can explore completely new ground.

Sir Bob Reid has similar instincts:

It's vital that you engage young business people's sense of adventure. You must send them out to do things which are beyond them and then be patient with them as they learn. You must invest in risk.

When you catch yourself saying things like "I couldn't possibly do it like that," you may be becoming set in your learning ways. To rediscover a spirit of adventure, seek out some simple, not too challenging but significantly different ways of doing things.

Try this simple exercise to get you in the right frame of mind. Sit on a chair with your knees out to the front and your hands by your side. Cross your legs. Uncross them. Cross them again. What do you notice? Did you cross the same leg over the other each time? If so, why? Now, cross your legs the other way. Stand up. Fold your arms over your chest. Let your arms drop down by your side. Refold them. Let them drop again. Did you cross the same arm over the other each time? Now, cross your arms the other way. Was it easy?

Most people naturally cross their leading leg over the other one when they cross their legs, but find it very easy to do it the other way round. With arms, most people find the opposite crossing a little more difficult, but can easily learn it. You can, in fact, almost feel your brain working out the new sense of cross-laterality as you do this! Crossing your arms the unnatural way is an image of what is involved when you try to relearn your adventurous spirit.

Here are some more simple ideas:

◆ Ask your partner or a friend to arrange an evening out with you, doing something of their choice, when all you know is what time you need to meet up.
◆ Try a different mode of transport to get to work for a day.
◆ Go to a concert of a kind of music that you don't normally listen to.
◆ Organize a visit to a business that is apparently nothing like yours and make a note of what you could learn for your place of work.

> *How adventurous are you feeling? If you need to rekindle your capacity for adventure, use some of the ideas above to help you. Then make a list of some ideas of your own to try.*

Successful learners in the Knowledge Age are like the merchant adventurers of old or the galactic explorers in the television series *Star Trek*. To boldly go where others may not have been, even if only in your mind, requires an inner strength. Elie Wiesel, Nobel prize winner and holocaust survivor, puts it like this:

We must understand that there can be no life without risk, and when our center is strong, everything else is secondary, even the risks.

To be successful, you need to keep the center of your being strong and fit. And the center is many-faceted, as I hope this book makes clear. For at the center is your ability to learn. If you are a competent learner, then all things are possible. The center will be most challenged when you come up against difficult or confusing things.

DEALING WITH DIFFICULTIES

Despite their good intentions, many people simply do not complete their learning because they hit some kind of difficulty and do not have a strategy for coping with it. This is equally true whether you are completing an MBA, learning how to put together a new piece of furniture, or coaching a local children's football team. Whatever the learning, there will be moments when you get stuck. You will feel frustration, anger, even despair. It is at these moments that you need some good coping strategies.

Intelligence, as Jean Piaget said many years ago, is "knowing what to do when you don't know what to do."

You probably know the popular television game show in the UK—exported to the US and other countries—called *Who Wants to Be a Millionaire?* Contestants are tested on their knowledge and each time they answer a question correctly, the prize money doubles until it reaches the magic figure of one million. As you can imagine, the atmosphere becomes more and more tense as the show progresses. It is, in fact, a good example of learning under pressure. If contestants are stuck, they can get help by telephoning a friend, asking the audience, or going 50:50, reducing the possibilities to two of the four options. The first two strategies involve getting support from someone else, while the third reduces the odds somewhat. It is still up to the contestant to reject or accept the advice they get, but the problem has been shared.

There are some useful tips for the lifelong learner here! When you get stuck you need to have good strategies for sticking with the problem. As the saying goes, there is no gain without pain. And this is equally true for learning.

The Swedish company Celemi lists "competence-enhancing customers" as one of the measurements on its Intangible Assets Monitor under the heading "Our people." The implication is quite clear. If your staff have lived through a difficult and challenging assignment with a client, they will be the stronger for it.

10 things to do when learning gets difficult

1   Stop what you are doing and have a complete break.
2   Think back to what you did the last time you got stuck like this.
3   Make a map or list in which you outline what your options are.
4   Talk to a friend about it to ask them what they would do.

5   Use a book to help you find a way through.
6   Use the internet to help you discover an answer.
7   Take some exercise and see if a solution comes to you.
8   Leave it. Go to bed. Tell yourself before you go to sleep that you will find a way through the problem.
9   Try doing whatever you are doing in a completely different location.
10   Think of as many questions as you can which, if answered, might help you to work things out.

HANDLING CONFUSION

It was American management guru Tom Peters who said, "If you're not confused, you're not thinking clearly." He may well have had today's rapidly changing society in mind. We are not living in an *A* to *B* world. It is much more likely that we will go from *D* to *H* via *Z*—and that we will be confused. The rules seem to change so rapidly that where one style of marketing is acceptable one day, the next week it is apparently not.

Perhaps it was always like this, as a statement by the sixteenth-century Englishman Sir Francis Bacon suggests: "We rise to great heights by a winding staircase." I suspect that learning has always involved messiness and confusion. In fact, my hunch is that those who are most at ease with uncertainty or confusion are the best learners.

If you have a set of rules, you need people who are good at following rules. But, the game of learning has a number of wild cards in its pack. Like Chance cards in Monopoly, they suddenly change the rules. What do you do when all the computer systems fail and you only have your presentation in electronic form? What do you do when you suddenly find yourself without a piece of equipment on which you normally rely? Can you cope when a senior colleague becomes ill and you have to stand in for her? It is in these situations that the ability to learn how to learn is essential. These are the really important learning experiences.

British management guru Charles Handy reminds us that when you ask most senior executives to remember their most important learning experiences, they will talk "of the time when continuity ran out on them, when they had no past experience to fall back on, no rules or handbook. They survived, however and came back stronger and more adaptable in mind and heart."

What do you do when things get really confusing? Use the ideas below and any of your own to apply to a real-life situation that is confusing you.

---

10 things to do when you are really confused

1   Stay calm.
2   Be true to yourself and remind yourself of your original objective.
3   Think of three different ways of approaching the situation and see if one of them is helpful.
4   Imagine what a practical or theoretical person (whichever you are less of) would do in the situation.
5   Go and watch carefully while someone else tackles the same issue and learn from them. (Remember, it is not cheating but a sign of intelligence to imitate others.)
6   Find out what experts in the field do in this situation by telephoning them, emailing them, or looking it up in a book.
7   Ask someone who apparently knows nothing about the details of what you are doing but who may inject some common-sense advice or get you thinking differently.
8   Search for guidance on the internet.
9   Come back to the problem at a different time of day.
10   Ponder whether it is the right thing to be continuing with your learning: occasionally it will be smarter to reflect on what you have learned and do something else.

Some people consciously create difficulty. Joyce Taylor is a good case in point. She says:

I actively enjoy difficulty and stress, indeed I create it by leaving things to the last minute.

By doing this, Joyce finds that she can be more creative. I share her approach, finding that, provided I have set my mind to process a problem or issue, I am much more likely to find an imaginative approach if I keep myself open to different possibilities for as long as possible.

In the next chapter you can find out more about how to harness your creativity, and in Part III you can read more about how to use your learning to help you adapt and change.

RESILIENCE—IN A NUTSHELL

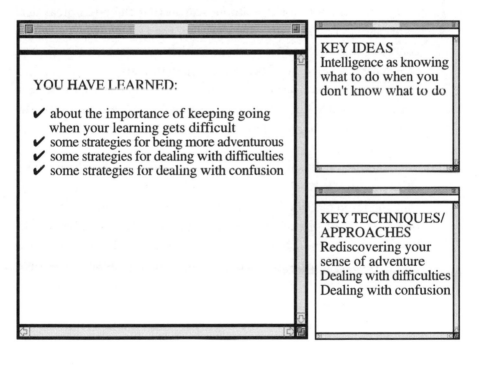

YOU HAVE LEARNED:

✔ about the importance of keeping going when your learning gets difficult
✔ some strategies for being more adventurous
✔ some strategies for dealing with difficulties
✔ some strategies for dealing with confusion

KEY IDEAS
Intelligence as knowing what to do when you don't know what to do

KEY TECHNIQUES/
APPROACHES
Rediscovering your sense of adventure
Dealing with difficulties
Dealing with confusion

9

Harnessing Your Creativity

THIS IS GOING TO BE A SLIGHTLY LONGER CHAPTER THAN SOME OF THE others in this book, for the simple reason that there is a great deal to be said about creativity and learning. For far too long, these two concepts have been dealt with as if they were unconnected. Yet, creativity is a key part of being a competent learner.

To help you see this, let me recap on two areas that you have already learned about that particularly relate to your creativity: the theory that your brain is divided into halves, and the brain's love of patterns.

You have already seen that there is considerable evidence that there are two "halves" to your brain, a left and a right side. It seems that the left-hand side is mainly responsible for language and number. It tends to process information logically. The right-hand side, however, takes a more holistic view of information. It enjoys patterns and is probably involved when you are thinking laterally. The right side is, not surprisingly, seen as the more creative of the two halves.

In very general terms, women tend to be right brained and men to be left brained. As with many findings about the brain, this kind of generalization needs to be treated with caution. Interestingly, it seems that the corpus callosum, the part of the brain connecting the two halves, is slightly thicker in people whose right side of the brain is dominant. It is a reasonable speculation to suggest that people who realize their creativity fully are those who can use both sides of their brain most effectively. They manage to take a whole-brained view of the world.

Your brain's tendency to put things into familiar patterns can be unhelpful when you are trying to be creative. Your mind seeks to make connections to things it already "knows" and then to "file" the experiences accordingly. Oscar Wilde wittily enshrined this truism when he said, "Consistency is the last refuge of the unimaginative." But it was Edward de Bono who observed, some 30 years ago:

Insight, creativity and humor are so elusive because the mind is so efficient. The mind functions to create patterns out of its surroundings. As the patterns are used they become ever more firmly established.

In other words, we become set in our ways, unwilling to think about something in a different way. It was as result of this that De Bono developed the technique now widely known as lateral thinking, some examples of which you will explore in this chapter.

There is a real sense in which, when it comes to releasing our creativity, we have to unlearn much of what we have picked up in our lives to date. We need to rethink what is meant by being creative and to find out the best way of creating the conditions in which we can learn to think more creatively.

There is one area of brain science that is particularly interesting with regard to creativity and learning. It is known as the "state of flow." Many of you will have had an experience of flow, when you are so caught up in a task that time ceases to matter. Perhaps you found this state when you were wholly engaged in writing something, or painting, or decorating, or involved in a soul-searching discussion. Or, perhaps you achieved it when you were deep in thought, or meditating, or jogging, with your mind able to reach deep inside itself as you pound along. The idea of the state of flow was first described by American scientist Mihalyi Csikszentmihalyi. You may also have heard this kind of experience referred to as being in the "alpha state."

The brain chemistry behind this idea is reasonably straightforward. Essentially, your brain runs at four different "speeds." You could think of it as four different gears in a car. The speeds are in fact different brain waves, called alpha, beta, theta, and delta. Your brain "transmits" different electrical impulses depending on what it is doing. If you were to measure these with something called an electroencephalograph, you would see that the different waves operate at different cycles per second.

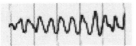

Alpha wave

Beta wave

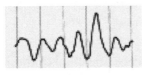

Theta wave

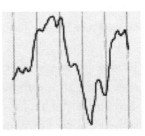

Delta wave

Beta waves are the fastest and delta the slowest. For example, when you are asleep your brain is operating most slowly. When you first go to sleep, it is producing theta waves at four to seven cycles per second. This is when you can almost feel your brain processing the experiences of the day, when you often have night thoughts and need to have a notepad by the bed to scribble them down. As you go into a deeper sleep, your brain slows down still further to as low as half a cycle per second or delta waves.

At work, your brain will be predominantly producing beta waves, somewhere between 13 and 25 cycles per second. This is the predominant daytime state of talking, thinking, problem solving, and all the tasks of a typical day.

However, it is the alpha state, some 8 to 12 waves per second, that we are increasingly realizing is very important. It is when many people have their best ideas, when your imagination is really working. Some people manage to reach this state easily, for example, in a really good creative session such as the one described in the day in the life of Annie's brain. Others need consciously to seek to lower the speed of their busy daytime brain, through techniques such as brain gym, autogenic training, yoga, or other methods of relaxation. Or, it could be through really concentrated effort that you somehow, to use the language of driving again, shift your mind up a gear and find its most creative speed.

There is one chemical in the brain that may be of particular interest if we are looking to provide fuel for our minds: gamma-aminobutyric acid. It appears that this neurotransmitter helps your brain to lock out unwanted stimuli and focus on what it wants to do. We secrete this chemical when we are in a state of flow, absorbed in a task. It seems that the chemical affects the membrane of neurons so that they will only respond to chosen stimuli. This helps to explain why, when you are totally engaged in learning something, you fail to hear other people's noise. We also secrete gamma-aminobutyric acid during the night, which offers some insight into why you can switch off from noises that might otherwise disturb you.

INSPIRATION, IDEAS, AND LEARNING

Just occasionally, like Archimedes in his bath all those years ago, we are suddenly blessed with a moment of inspiration. You may remember that he had been struggling to work out how to prove that the emperor's crown was made of gold. To do this, he had to be sure of the density and weight of the metal used in the crown. Sinking into his bath after another fruitless session in his workshop, history has it that he noticed how his body displaced water. He cried "*Eureka!*" as inspiration suddenly arrived: he had realized that the weight of the water displaced was the weight of the body that had displaced it.

All of us are occasionally capable of an "aha!" moment, when a new idea is born. Our learning in these situations is mysterious and unpredictable. We often do not know how we have had a new idea. To begin to understand this area a little, we will need to speculate about what Archimedes was doing before he took his bath. How many different ways of working out the amount of gold in the emperor's crown had he tried? Did his insight arrive precisely because he was relaxing in a bath rather than laboring away in his workshop? What was it about his state of mind that made him receptive to new thinking?

The answers to these questions are complex, but worth pursuing further. By exploring them, we may be able to understand more about the close connection between learning and creativity. Knowing how to harness your own creativity is one of the most important aspects of learning to learn. For in these "aha!" moments, there is no doubt that your mind is fully powered up and somehow operating in another gear.

Creativity has only recently begun to be seen as part of learning. The kind of learning valued in IQ tests held sway in schools and colleges for much of the twentieth century; to a large extent it still does. In this view of education, creativity is consigned to art, design, and music. Very little connection is made between the kind of innovation and entrepreneurial thought that is needed in business and the approach to learning being adopted by schools.

The omission of creativity from the school curriculum had become so serious that one of the first acts of the Blair government after it came to power in Britain in 1997 was to set up a national advisory committee on creative and cultural education. As one of the members of this committee, Professor Susan Greenfield, puts it:

Original thought and respect for originality of others must surely lie at the heart, not just of creativity, but also individuality—our only chance of twenty-first-century escape from zombie-ness.

In too many schools and in too many tests, there is one right answer to every question or problem. In life, especially in a world of rapid change, there is rarely one simple answer. There are normally too many complex issues for a single point of view to suffice. And this is quite apart from the fact that we know that human beings have many more intelligences than the linguistic and mathematical elements traditionally associated with IQ.

Some people talk of a separate creative intelligence, but this misses the point. It suggests that creativity is an isolated aspect of the way we act. I am convinced that it is a much more pervasive attribute, an attitude of mind that can be applied to all we do.

Creativity is increasingly being sought after as a key aspect of the way you learn and perform. As the authoritative Alan

Greenspan, chairman of the US Federal Reserve Board, wrote recently in the *Wall Street Journal*:

Virtually unimaginable half a century ago was the extent to which concepts and ideas would substitute for physical resources and human brawn in the production of goods and services.

You can create value out of thin air if you can think creatively.

There is a myth that you are born creative, that creativity is something you either do or do not have. While this clearly applies to particular aspects—in music and other arts, for example—it is untrue that you cannot learn to be more creative. It is quite possible to make creativity a way of being.

As French scientist Louis Pasteur put it at the beginning of the nineteenth century: "Chance favors only the prepared mind." You need to ensure that your mind is prepared so that it is more likely to enjoy those surges of power called inspiration.

THE CHARACTERISTICS OF CREATIVE PEOPLE

If creativity has been misunderstood, then so too has the notion of what it is to be creative. It has been assumed that only artists, musicians, and media people are creative. This is not the case.

It is axiomatic of the idea of being creative that no one person's list of characteristics will look the same as another's. For what it is worth, here are the kind of words and phrases I associate with being creative:

Risk taking	Willing to see many perspectives
Challenging	Not overcontrolling
Happy to live with uncertainty	Not too bound by social pressure
Happy to live with complexity	Happy to be different
Openness	In touch with emotions
Exploring	Playful
Able to suspend judgment	Irreverent

You can see from a list like this that this kind of quality is desirable in many business sectors. Within organizations, creative people are increasingly being referred to as intrapreneurs and being given the support and encouragement they need to turn their ideas into new products and services. Individuals are becoming brands in their own right. Richard Branson was an early example of this phenomenon, which is now becoming much more widespread.

Markets are dominated by ideas that, in John Grant's words, "catch on like viruses." Good recent examples of these are products such as the iMac, Pokemon, Volkswagen's New Beetle, Starbucks, Hotmail, and concepts like "organic" and "wired."

What do you think? What would your list of characteristics look like? Were you taught to be creative at school or college? Are you taught to be creative at work?
Who are the most creative people you know at work? At home? What makes them stand out?
Are you actively seeking to acquire some of the characteristics listed above?
What are you doing to identify the intrapreneurs within your organization?
What viral products or concepts have caught your imagination recently?

THE VALUE OF IDEAS

The capacity to learn and the capacity to generate ideas are linked to our prosperity. If we want to be smarter and more successful, we will want to know more about these processes.

My own view is that to be creative, you need both concentrated periods of activity and concentrated periods of apparent inactivity. It is possible to achieve flow in both situations, and it is one of the enjoyable mysteries of creativity that you never know when a great thought is going to come to fruition.

While I was writing this book, I interviewed a number of business leaders from a range of organizations. I asked them all where they had their best ideas. Not one of them said that they had their best ideas at work. Many of them gathered inspiration from those around them and from their work outside their main job. Each of them, in different ways, talked about moments of flow or relaxation when they were elsewhere. They often described the social processes in nurturing ideas.

Colin Marshall is clear about his creativity:

Good ideas come from many inspirational sources, but usually result from confronting a problem from all angles to find a solution. To capture a good idea the answer is to share it with somebody else whose judgment and integrity you trust. If the idea is really good, he or she will not let you get away with not seeing it through.

Zoe van Zwanenberg of the Scottish Leadership Foundation says:

My best ideas often come out of a conversation. Someone triggers something off. Or it's from watching. I remember observing the Royal Ballet on tour in China. While I was watching their principals go through their daily class with all the junior dancers watching, I suddenly saw how this could be translated into the organizations I knew.

Joyce Taylor told me:

I generally get my best ideas when there is space, at home or on a walk or at night.

For Neil Chambers, director of London's Natural History Museum, it is travel "to get ideas, often sifting through them on journeys and then kicking them around with key colleagues on my return." Sir Bob Reid has his best ideas "after a period of minimal activity or when I am taking part in physical activity." And most of Jayne-Anne Gadhia's best ideas come when she is running or in the shower.
Hilary Cropper says:

I have ideas in all kinds of places. I suddenly see an opportunity. But I don't do it on my own. Invariably it involves teams of people. I describe a problem to someone else and this helps me to organize my thoughts.

A different place and a different pace seem to be key elements of effective idea creation. Whatever the method adopted, it is clear that many people's working environment does little to stimulate their creativity. See page 159 for ideas on how you can do this.

As ever, we need to be careful about making generalizations, but it would be safe to say that for many people, finding ways of getting into the alpha state more often, both at work and at home, is beneficial to their creativity.

And in today's climate, as David Meier puts it:

The greatest threat to any organization is not the lack of ability or resources, but the failure of imagination.

MULTIPLE INTELLIGENCES

More than anyone, psychologist Howard Gardner has revolutionized the concept of intelligence by introducing the idea that there is not one but eight intelligences. Interestingly, Gardner started in the 1980s with seven, introduced an eighth, the naturalist intelligence, in the 1990s, and has recently been toying with a ninth, existential intelligence.

Gardner's theory of multiple intelligences is a profoundly important link in the chain between learning and creativity. If you accept that each person has many intelligences, it is an easy step to assume that being creative means being able to harness the fullest potential of each of your intelligences.

By suggesting that there are many intelligences, Gardner has given us an implicit definition of creativity that moves us away from the act of creating a new artistic product toward the notion that each of us has the potential to develop each of our intelligences. Creativity becomes much more a state of being than a privileged artistic activity. Learning and creativity are created by dint of any competent learner wanting to be able to harness their potential in as many of their intelligence areas as possible.

While Howard Gardner has argued for seven, then eight, and most recently nine intelligences, I believe that there are ten. But, whether I am right or wrong, what is important is that there is more than the one intelligence that has dominated so much of western thought, IQ.

Learning to learn: releasing your creativity

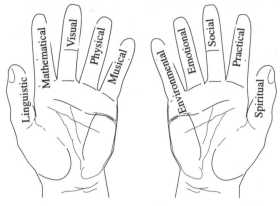

Here are some simple descriptions of the different characteristics of my ten intelligences. Just by reading them, you will probably be able to see where you have particular strengths and where you are less confident. You may well find several intelligences with which you immediately identify. You may also find bits of some descriptions that seem to apply to you while some elements do not. They are only meant as a guide, to begin to help you see the various facets of your mind that can contribute to your overall success.

Linguistic

You like words and stories. Word play intrigues you. You are probably the kind of person who enjoys proofreading and has a distinct view of what is correct or sloppy use of language. You are an avid reader. You express yourself with clarity and have a good vocabulary. You probably enjoyed learning languages and literature at school and may have gone on to study these at a higher level. You enjoy writing and may well be able to speak and write more than one language. You may be able to remember lists of words and remember and tell good stories.

Mathematical

You like figures and abstract problems. You like to understand the relationships between different things and are probably the sort of person who likes to know how things work and fix them when they go wrong. You may well enjoy doing brainteasers and playing chess or Trivial Pursuit. You probably enjoyed learning mathematics at school. You like argument and evidence. You enjoy patterns, categories, and systems. You probably make lists at home and at work and tick off the things you manage to achieve. You like logical order. You may well enjoy reading financial figures, although this is not always the case.

(My mathematical intelligence is based on Gardner's logical-mathematical. Visual and mathematical together are the ones that are rewarded in IQ tests and tests derived from them. These two intelligences have dominated much of the literature of success and performance for a century, to the exclusion of the others.)

Visual

You like pictures and shapes. You notice color, form, and texture. You probably make use of diagrams, maps, and doodles when you are in meetings, listening to others, or simply thinking on your own. You probably use pictures to help you remember things. You may well be able to draw, paint, or sculpt. You probably spent time in the arts department at school. You may enjoy visiting galleries and noticing architecture or landscape. You like maps and cartoons and prefer to be supported by material that is illustrated rather than relying on the written word.

Physical

You like to work with your body and to use your hands. You enjoy physical exercise and probably take part in sporting or dance activity of some kind, either now or in the past. You are the kind of person who gets up on your feet at the first opportunity when in a group meeting at work or on a dance floor at a party. You like to handle things directly and enjoy the sensation of new experiences. You may well use your body to aid communication, waving your hands, gesturing with your shoulders, and using facial expressions to augment the meaning of what you are saying. You probably enjoy mime and games like charades. You like to learn by doing and you are the first to roll up your sleeves and get on with things.

Musical

You like sounds and rhythms. You are also interested in the tonal qualities of different sounds and can probably pick out different instruments when you listen to music. You may have enjoyed singing and listening to music from an early age. You may well be actively involved in making music and will almost certainly enjoy going to concerts and listening to music at home and on journeys. You have a good sense of rhythm and can remember songs and melodies well. You recall advertisements mainly for their music. You often hum to yourself and can easily be emotionally transported by a piece of music. Music acts powerfully on your moods.

Emotional

You like to look within yourself, an instinct that has you continually questing for self-knowledge. You are constantly analyzing your strengths and weaknesses and setting goals to do something to improve yourself. You may well keep notes or a diary or personal log of your experiences, moods, and thoughts. You explore those situations that give you pleasure and those that cause pain, and seek to act accordingly. You understand and manage your own emotions well. You enjoy having time to think and reflect. You may well have pursued some kind of counseling or self-improvement activity.

(This intelligence, made famous by Daniel Goleman, develops the idea of Gardner's intrapersonal intelligence.)

Social

You like to be with and understand other people. Not surprisingly, you enjoy parties, meetings, team games, and any gregarious activities. You have the ability to understand and relate to other people. You can read the moods and plans of others, so that people tend to seek you out when they need advice. You are often the person who is called on to sort out difficult situations and resolve differences of opinion. You have a number of close friends with whom you share a great deal. You show high levels of empathy with others. You like talking over people's problems and people turn to you to be their coach, buddy, mentor, and critical friend.

(This is based on Gardner's interpersonal intelligence.)

Environmental

You like the natural world. You see meaning and patterns in nature that pass others by. You have a good knowledge of plants, animals, and land-scape, knowing not just names but the characteristics of the elements of the world around you. You probably have or have had pets. At school, you may well have enjoyed botany, zoology, and biology. You like being outside and when walking are a fountain of knowledge about what is going on in nature. You take a keen interest in your own home environment, inside and outside. You notice the weather and the seasons and may be deeply affected by them. You know a fair amount about the workings of your own body. You enjoy classifying species.

(This is based on Gardner's naturalist intelligence, which he added later to his original seven intelligences.)

Spiritual

You like to deal with the fundamental questions of existence. You are the kind of person of who, when faced with difficult issues, will want to act according to your principles, possibly questioning the normal ways of behaving in the situation in which you find your-self. You seek constantly to explore your whole self and to heal those parts that seem not to be well. You are interested in values. You will probably hold particularly well-developed beliefs but may not practice any particular religious faith. You think about issues of duty. You tend to see some value in different sides of an argument. You may well be involved in some kind of community service. You would be ready to stand up and be counted for what you believe in.

(This intelligence has been suggested by Danah Zohar and Ian Marshall.)

Practical

You like making things happen. You have the capacity to sort things out and are often called on to fix, mend, or assemble things. Where others talk about what needs to be done, you prefer to get on and do it. You enjoy difficult or stressful situations because of your ability to come up with workable solutions. When things go wrong you are continually thinking of useful ideas to help others. You like to explain by doing. You constantly want to put theory into practice. You may well enjoy gardening and DIY. At school you enjoyed practical subjects. In domestic life you are the person who is happy to spend hours assembling flat-packed goods of all kinds. As a child you were always taking things apart to see how they worked. You enjoy seeing the inner workings of many items.

(This intelligence has been suggested by various thinkers, including Charles Handy and Robert Sternberg.)

If linguistic and mathematical intelligences were the key ones for the twentieth century, there is a strong case that emotional, social, and spiritual intelligences will be critical in the twenty-first century. To power up your mind fully, of course, it will be helpful for you to seek to develop all your intelligences, and, of course, your ability to learn how to learn.

By now, you might be wondering whether these different kinds of intelligence relate to different areas of the brain. The answer to this is that they don't. The brain, as you are discovering, is almost infinitely plastic and flexible.

Although we now know that certain aspects of the brain are largely responsible for specific activities, for example Wernicke's and Broca's areas for language and a small area in the temple for an aspect of musical appreciation, we also know that these areas are probably only part of a much more complex pattern of brain activity. In other words, you cannot do a map of the brain that correlates with intelligences.

Clearly, as we grow up, we discover that we have these intelligences in different states of development. Some of us are musical, some have powerful visual senses. Some of us are very good at visualizing, some very good with people. But these intelligences are not set in stone, they can be acquired to a considerable extent. We all inherit certain characteristics—our nature—but can develop considerably—our nurture. Most of us can develop all the intelligences considerably, even if we cannot become world beaters in every area.

Each of your ten intelligences can help you be more successful at work and at home. To be fully creatively developed, you need to realize your potential in as many of your intelligences as possible.

THE MULTIPLE INTELLIGENCE WORKPLACE

Remember the underlying argument of this section, that a prime source of competitive advantage in a business is its capacity to release the creativity of its employees. From what we know about how this is done, we can say with growing certainty that it will be likely to be achieved if there is a culture in which each employee is encouraged to develop their full potential.

Remember, too, that releasing your creativity is a key component of learning to learn, and therefore of developing your natural intelligence. When the Campaign for Learning asked the British public about their attitudes to learning, the phrase "Discover the hidden talents within you" was found to be the one most likely to motivate them.

At first glance, you may not immediately see how the idea of multiple intelligences can be applied to the workplace. How could it be advantageous, for example, to develop someone's musical or physical intelligence at work, unless you are in the music or leisure industries? Surely, this is what you learn at school or at home.

Look at the chart opposite. Use it to work out what might be different if you really wanted to help people harness more of their intelligences in your workplace.

Intelligence	Environment	People and learning	Internal communications	Rewards	Management structures
Linguistic				Use stories to motivate people to understand where the business is going	
Mathematical			Use puzzles and games to help people grasp issues such as the need to cut costs		
Visual			Use pictures, posters, cartoons, screensavers, and computer graphics to communicate		
Physical	Provide a gym and encourage employees to take up yoga				
Musical	Use music to create mood in meetings, workshops and social areas				
Emotional					Focus on the development of emotional intelligence as a key area of management competence
Social	Create spaces where employees can "flock" and share ideas				
Environmental	Invest heavily in plants inside and create external environments demonstrating interest in the natural world				
Spiritual					Be open about the values of the business and allow individuals to take ethical positions
Practical		Recognize that many people prefer to learn through doing			

Setting out your intention to harness the full range of people's talents gives out strong cultural messages to your workforce. When Jayne-Anne Gadhia set up Virgin One Account, she had to persuade people in good jobs in other more traditional financial services companies to come and work for her. The idea that Virgin One would be a more creative environment and one in which individuals would realize more of their potential was an attractive element of the package for them.

As more and more businesses become service and not manufacturing based, being a multiple intelligence workplace becomes more and more important.

Jonas Ridderstråle and Kjell Nordstrom, the Swedish authors of the bestselling *Funky Business*, are convinced that "the only thing that now makes capital dance is talent."

Do you agree with them? Do you think that the multiple intelligence approach is helpful? How much of this happens in your own organization? What impact might it have on your business if your workplace became multiply intelligent?

BARRIERS TO CREATIVITY

You will have heard of the idea of the learning organization, but what about the creative organization? It has many of the characteristics of creative people listed on page 149. It is an organization where the culture is one of constantly celebrating the value of ideas. For, as Charles Browder said:

A new idea is delicate. It can be killed by a sneer or a yawn, it can be stabbed to death by a quip and worried to death by a frown on the right man's brow.

Creative organizations understand the barriers to creativity and know how to overcome them. I think of these barriers as the seven deadly sins because they all, rather conveniently, begin with the letter S:

School
Sneering
Social pressure
Status quo
Standardization
Silos
Suits

When I refer to *school*, I am really referring to the idea that there is one right answer and that IQ dominates.

Sneering is still prevalent in organizations. It is the absolute enemy of creativity. This is partly why brainstorming is as successful as it is: it forces participants to delay their critical judgment or, at worst, sneers.

Social pressure can take many forms. Often, it is a prevailing orthodoxy, such as the belief that the only way to solve problems is by spending very long hours on them. It could be a view that it can never be right to use consultants for some jobs or, conversely, that it is always right to use them. In some organizations the social pressure is quite simple: to do what you are told to do by those superior to you. I can think of organizations where it is considered quite acceptable to pull individuals out of longstanding commitments, at short notice, for no good business reason, simply because it suits a very senior manager to gather a particular group of people together at that time.

Adhering to the *status quo* is not consistent with the essence of creative thinking and leads to many organizations going out of business. When you hear phrases like "But we've always done it like this," you know that there are going to be limiting boundaries to what is being thought through. This tendency is often linked to a view that is sometimes referred to as "not invented here."

By *standardization*, I mean that the brain's tendency to organize into the patterns it feels comfortable with makes it unlikely to want to go back to basics and rethink structures completely. In many cases, this may be exactly what is required!

Silos are airtight containers or deep pits for storing things. As such, they suggest organizations made up of isolated, unconnected departments or sections. The culture of these places is jealously to guard knowledge and compete more aggressively in a mythical internal market than in the real world of the organization's customers. Such cultures are enjoyed by "command-and-control" thinkers. They are the places in which people who are not open to new ideas like to feel comfortable.

And finally *suits*. I have got nothing against suits personally; in fact I rather like them. During my own career I have quite consciously worn particular suits and ties to ensure that those I am trying to persuade are at least not going to be put off by the superficialities of what I am wearing. Sometimes it is easier to speak radical thoughts if you are dressed in the clothes of the "tribe" with which you are working—we are less threatened and our minds are therefore more receptive to new ideas.

In fact, an environment of relentless jeans and t-shirts can be just as oppressively uniform as rows of suits. However, I use suits here to suggest the tyranny of a place in which everything is subordinated to an imagined view of what it is appropriate for people to wear, without any consideration for the preferences of individuals or the nature of the work being undertaken. In the current business environment, clothes themselves have become an interestingly unreliable way of judging creativity. Dress-down Fridays provide freedom for some and embarrassment for others.

Interestingly, many of the world's largest consultancies are now issuing guidance on appropriate dress-down codes for dealing with clients. The results of dressing down can be quite dreadful as confused consultants, without the certainty of their suits, opt for their equally offputting "executive leisure wear." The shape of your shoe, the type of shoulder bag you carry, and the style of shirt you choose all, of course, give out powerful messages in today's brand-conscious environment.

Do you agree with these ideas? Have you encountered these or similar barriers in your workplace? Can you think of examples from your own experience of any of these "serious sins"? If so, what could you do to prevent it happening?

Can you think of other ways in which people's creativity can be undermined?

How do you dress at work? To what extent do you think it is appropriate for employees to wear what they want for business? Do you welcome the current move away from the suit?

MAKING CONNECTIONS

There are very few really new ideas. Most of the time they are creative combinations of existing ideas:

◆ The idea of the wheel + the invention of steel + the invention of steam power = the railway.
◆ The letter + the wordprocessor + the modem = email.
◆ The radio + the cassette player + a set of headphones = the Sony Walkman.
◆ The idea of a very big bookshop + the internet = Amazon.com.
◆ Our tendency to leave everything to the last second + the idea of the one-stop shop + the internet = Lastminute.com.
◆ The idea of the university + new technologies = the virtual or corporate university.
◆ The old way of washing clothes with a mangle and a scrubbing board + modern technology with two tubs rotating in opposite directions = the latest Dyson washing machine.

As MIT's Nicholas Negroponte puts it:

New ideas come from differences. They come from having different perspectives and juxtaposing different theories.

American poet Robert Frost has it even more succinctly: "An idea is a feat of association."

Will Hutton, chief executive of the Industrial Society, expands on this further:

I have the kind of mind which makes connections. Nothing is original. I am self-confident in making unusual links. You need to dare to make a connection and be prepared for hostile reactions as you take people into new territory.

To make it more likely that people will make connections and therefore have good ideas that will be commercially and socially beneficial, there are three simple ways of encouraging this art of making connections in the workplace: using dialog, moving outside your field on a regular basis, and learning to think in terms of connections.

Using dialog as a way of life

If people are to make connections, they need to talk to each other. The pace of life, linked to the fact that many people in offices are largely glued to the computer screen on their desk, means that communication is ever more fragmented and one way. The same is true at home. Where it was once common for families to sit down and eat breakfast and supper together, this important social occasion is virtually a thing of the past in most households.

Many organizations are beginning to recognize that to harness the creativity of their employees, they need to create structures that encourage dialog. British Airways is one. As Colin Marshall puts it:

The most interesting and stimulating way of learning is from direct dialog with other people, whether in an educational context or straightforward business debate.

Dialog assumes that there is no one right answer. It assumes that solutions and truth may lie somewhere in the middle of two apparently conflicting points of view. Dialog encourages engagement and commitment. It is a two-way process in which speaking and listening are equally valued. In their excellent book *Executive EQ*, Robert Cooper and Ayman Sawaf memorably describe dialog as "the free flowing of meaning between people."

For dialog to take place, especially if it is to be accompanied by any eating or drinking—which, of course, it often is—it is helpful to have round tables. And, hey presto, you have invented the Creative Café. Café-style communication is becoming increasingly common. Café spaces are being planned into corporate architecture and into training and conference facilities. I have found that this can work very well at all levels of business life.

A little while ago, with the specialist learning and communications company Purple Works, the Campaign for Learning designed a café experience for about 100 people from right across the UK-based energy and telecommunications company National Grid. The purpose of the event was to encourage individuals to share their perceptions of where the company had come from, where it was going to, and what learning it needed to help it become a world-class company.

Around the tables sat the chairman of the company, David Jefferies, some of his board, some influential individuals not directly connected with National Grid, senior staff, engineers, trade unionists, and the linesmen who climb up the towers when storms cause trees to fall on them. On each table there was a circular learning mat, designed to fit it like a tablecloth. On each learning mat we placed a series of images, statements, charts, and questions designed to stimulate dialog. The feedback from this café-style approach was that it was far more engaging and far more satisfying than other forms of communication that they had experienced. It was also felt to be a genuine and realistic way for people with different kinds of responsibility and levels of seniority to communicate with each other.

The National Grid experience was designed as a special event. However, for the dialog approach to be really effective, it needs to become a way of life within an organization.

My own hunch is that there is more opportunity for creativity in dialog than in brainstorming, which has long been associated with the generation of ideas.

What do you think? How much do you use dialog in your organization?

Moving outside your field

While it is essential to encourage a free flow of meaning within your organization, it is equally important to have ways of encouraging a flow of ideas from the outside.

When Neil Chambers, director of London's Natural History Museum, first joined the museum, he was concerned to improve the ways in which the museum dealt with visitors. He decided to send all his senior staff on Disney's quality service course in Orlando. Disney World may not seem very similar to a natural history museum, but Neil reckoned that his staff would make creative connections to the customer care offered by the leisure industry—and that is exactly what they did. If you go to the London museum now you can also see a move toward edutainment of which Walt Disney would have been proud.

Sir Michael Bichard, Permanent Secretary at the British Department for Education and Employment, is passionate about moving out of the traditional field of the civil service:

I learn and enhance my creativity by meeting people. I invest as much time as possible in visiting projects. I find I pick up good ideas that are not fully developed and I am able to work on them until they are fully formed and of potentially national impact.

Thinking like this is essential in a creative organization. Great Ormond Street, London's famous children's hospital, recently discovered there was much it could learn from Formula One pit stop tire and fuel changes when it came to improving its systems for intensive care beds! Often, there is no training course available to meet a very specific identified need, and for organizations determined to improve all aspects of their operations continuously, getting out and seeing how other organizations do things is essential. It is often helpful to visit enterprises that are not like yours, but where some aspect of their operation might stimulate your creativity. So, a bank might look at how a leisure attraction deals with its customers, a manufacturing business might look at systems in a service industry, and so on.

The same approach works very well for individuals looking for new thinking about the way they manage aspects of their work. In this case, it might be that an individual could choose to find out more about how people from very different organizations manage people, run meetings, handle internal communications, etc.

As well as going out to see how other people do things, it can be very helpful to invite people in to work with you. In some organizations this is described as being a "critical friend." It is a role I have played myself with British Telecom. As part of the process of developing a major communication project, FutureTalk, the company was keen to have a trusted outsider who would offer constructive challenge and feedback as the creative team moved from idea to product and then into the marketplace. In this case I knew a reasonable amount about the particular project, as it covered communication and learning, but the same approach would have worked even if I had known nothing at all.

Have you used the critical friend idea? If so, how did it help? If not, can you think of an aspect of your work that might benefit from it?

Sometimes, especially when you are at the early stage of the development of a project, it is helpful to go still further and quite deliberately involve someone who is from a very different line of work. I call this kind of person a "lay consultant." If your project was in the area of telecommunications, for example, you could involve a writer, an actor, or a speech therapist to work with you as a critical friend. Such a lay consultant's views are often invaluable in broadening and challenging assumptions.

Playing with connections

To help you get into the habit of making connections, there is a very simple game you can play that will help train your mind.

First, make a list of about 50 everyday household, workplace, and high street items, for example, game of Monopoly, pet dog, sycamore seed, chair, pencil, paperclip, desk, car, pedestrian, etc.

To begin with, you may like to put each one on a separate small piece of paper or card. Then, identify an aspect of your work or home life on which you wish to focus. Let's imagine that you choose to explore something that is an issue in all organizations: cutting your costs.

Pick one of your cards. Let's say you chose the game of Monopoly. For between 20 or 30 minutes, concentrate on finding connections between cost cutting and the game of Monopoly.

Try lots of different techniques:

◆   Working on your own and coming up with a list.
◆   Asking yourself questions about how they are similar in shape or colour or process or any other thing you can think of.
◆   Brainstorming.
◆   Focusing on one aspect of either of the two areas.
◆   Getting up, walking around, and seeing if the problem looks different when you are on your feet.

The kinds of ideas you might have come up with would include:

◆   Both use money.
◆   You go to jail if you don't pay up.
◆   There are risks involved.
◆   You "go round in circles" when playing Monopoly and when trying to save money.
◆   When you pass "Go" you get money and when you do something to cut costs you get money.

If at any time the connection you are making between the two items gives you an idea, capture it. What tends to happen is that to begin with the ideas are quite obvious. After a while the thinking starts to deepen. Someone might notice that the houses at one end of the board are cheaper than those at the other end. This could suggest to you that the best way of cutting costs would be for you to move offices to cheaper ones and make a significant saving, rather than spending so much of your time talking about making minor cuts.

Games like these are a good metaphor for what needs to happen in a creative organization. Peter Drucker talks of taking "a systematic leap into the unknown." Certainly there is much that is unknown, but equally there is much that can be done to make creativity more systematic.

Try this technique out on some of your most pressing business issues and see what happens.

CREATIVE THINKING

Edward De Bono has revolutionized the way we think creatively. It is 40 years since he invented the idea of lateral thinking, but many of his ideas still seem as fresh as ever. De Bono's approach is typified by his famous remark, "You cannot dig a hole in a different place by digging the same hole deeper." In other words, to think creatively you need to make new associations and find new ways of looking at things. You need to put down your spade, find a pick ax, and walk to another spot where perhaps you will have to remove the concrete first.

Here are seven practical ideas for thinking creatively, the first two taken from De Bono.

Capturing the interest

When you are looking closely at a problem, there is a great tendency to view it in black-and-white terms and so to reduce it to opposites. This tends to lead to closed thinking. By using the headings "Plus," "Minus," and "Interesting," it is possible to categorize ideas so as to keep things more open.

Take any idea or proposition—for example, that we should abolish all schools—and apply these words to it. It might look something like this:

+	−	Interesting
It would cost less in taxes. You could learn what you like. Etc.	Many teachers would lose their jobs. Children from poor families might suffer.	You could use the buildings for other things. Parents might get more involved.

As you can already see, the ideas in the third column are shaping up well.

Choose one of your own business issues and subject it to this way of thinking.

Wearing six hats

This classic De Bono approach is an excellent way of getting the most out of creative teams and is a gentle play on the saying "putting on your thinking cap." It recognizes that there are many different roles in the creative process and that it is sometimes helpful to be more explicit about this.

De Bono assumes that when a team is grappling with a problem, it may be helpful to be really clear about the different roles you can play. So, he suggests that you wear six differently colored hats and act according to the role that each one suggests.

White = You introduce neutral facts, figures and information.
Red = You put forward hunches, feeling and intuitions.
Black = You are logical and negative.
Yellow = You are logical and positive.
Green = You constantly come up with creative ideas for taking things forward.
Blue = You act as the conductor of the orchestra, concentrating on managing the process of coming up with ideas successfully.

There are all sorts of ways in which this can be used, but the simplest is just to play the roles that each hat suggests. You could add other colors and other roles. This technique could be used in a social setting or as a warm-up item to a more serious meeting.

Find a way of applying this approach in your own life. If you like the idea, you can read more about this in De Bono's classic book, Six Thinking Hats. Make sure you don't always wear the same hat!

Fuzzy thinking

At the start of this section I was speculating about what Archimedes had been doing before he slipped gratefully into his warm bath. Did the answer come to him because he had been wrestling so hard with his conscious mind about ways of checking on the gold in the crown? Or, did the answer somehow come to him because his mind was in a much more fuzzy state as he lay in the bath? Was bath-time a mechanism by which he managed to achieve a deeper thinking level, a state of flow perhaps?

We shall never know, of course. But there is strong empirical evidence from various inventors and artists that the fuzzier, gentler, "bath-time" state is an extremely fecund one for ideas. It seems likely that you need both the hard, concentrated engagement and the gentler, less focused approach, and that you need to be able to move between the two with ease.

As De Bono's idea of an "interesting" category demonstrates, it is always helpful when you can find a position that is between the extremes of such tyrannical opposites as "yes" and "no," "know" and "don't know."

In a world of complexity where I find myself increasingly uncertain and opposed to dogmatic positions, I find the intuition template below a helpful one to induce gentler, fuzzier approaches:

Certain about the solution	Strong hunch or intuition
Possible way forward that needs testing	Don't know what to do but happy to keep saying this

Think of a business issue you are wrestling with and use this template on it. Does it help?

Having hunches is like working in three rather than two dimensions. You are no longer so bound by the demands of time and place. You can see the problem from different perspectives.

By concentrating on the idea of the hunch, something very interesting happens to you and your relationship to time. You begin to dwell on an idea over a period, letting it roll around your head. People who have a hunch often tell you so and seek your involvement in thinking it through. As you mull something over, so you start to look at it from all sorts of different angles.

In a world increasingly dominated by deadlines and short-term performance regimes, we need to listen to our hunches and intuitions more, not less.

Jonas Ridderstråle and Kjell Nordstrom encapsulate this belief with a powerful metaphor: "We have to turn the workplace into a gas station for our brains, not only a racetrack."

Guy Claxton has explored the idea of "soft thinking" extensively in his writing. In his book, *Hare Brain, Tortoise Mind: Why Intelligence Increases When You Think Less*, he makes a compelling case for letting your mind work at different speeds. The book offers a wealth of insights into the complex process of learning to learn, for example, that the apparently contradictory sayings "Look before you leap" and "He who hesitates is lost" can both be true.

At various stages in this book, I have included practical suggestions for how you can seek to move from the stressful, time-dominated present into the fuzzier, but somehow more creatively focused world I am describing.

Creative organizations make time for people to find their creativity. In some consultancies it is, for example, becoming common-place for senior staff to be given time off after challenging assignments to recharge their batteries and to reflect on what they have learned.

One practical way of creating time at work is consciously to seek to undertake fewer projects in smaller teams. The larger the team, the more it is necessary to meet. The more functional meetings you have, the less time there is for fuzzier, more productive thinking and learning.

When Richard Branson creates a new business he does not subsume it within Virgin. While it benefits from the Virgin name, Branson has shown how much more creative it can be to keep teams small and focused and leave them space to create.

Interestingly, research has shown that you tend to come up with more creative ideas after the initial burst of ideas that you produce. This truth, linked to the idea that the world is becoming much more complex, explains why a fuzzier approach is increasingly helpful to have as part of your own toolkit of skills.

This is partly why I think that brainstorming is an overrated pastime. Edward de Bono stressed that the key element of the technique was the deferring of judgment. It is this important ingredient that allows the necessary space for creativity. Unfortunately, brainstorming has come to be used so routinely and with such time pressures that, in my experience, it can all too often simply be the pooling of the most banal and obvious ideas. It has been embraced by some organizations as a means of suggesting that they are creative and open to new ideas, when in fact it has become an example of rather uncreative communication. If you are brainstorming, then it is worth building in some quiet pauses for those who are not extraverts and giving individuals the chance to "speak" to themselves at a different speed.

So, while brainstorming can be extremely helpful, it needs time and the ideas it generates need to be subjected to some of the creative techniques you have been exploring in this section.

Do you manage to create time for fuzzy thinking in your business life? If so, how do you do it? If not, how might you do so?

Problem finding

Sometimes we think we are solving problems that do not really exist, except in our own minds. Or, at least, the way that the problem is phrased simply does not go to the core of the issue. In these situations, it can be helpful to reframe the problem in more abstract terms.

A good example of this was the "people's revolt" against rising fuel prices in Britain in 2000. By blockading fuel depots, a handful of protesters—farmers, hauliers, those living in rural areas—brought the country to a near standstill and the government was seen to be ill prepared for such an extraordinary turn of events.

At first sight, this was presented as if it were a problem of the Blair government being out of touch with the people. New Labour was seen as losing its popular instincts—people thought it could easily reduce the tax element of the cost of fuel in an otherwise buoyant market. Most of the press portrayed this as the problem, to which the answer was for the Prime Minister and Chancellor of the Exchequer to heed the voices of ordinary people and reduce the amount of tax on fuel. A few saw it as an expression of greed by the oil companies.

Reframe this problem in more abstract terms and it becomes a very different issue of sustainable development. The real problem suddenly becomes much clearer: How might a government per-suade people that paying more for fuel is the right thing to be doing if a commitment to the environment means that we all need to drive our cars less? The problem then becomes one of culture change. Creative energies can be focused on changing our percep-tion of the role of the car in our lives. By finding the real problem, you can create the real solution.

Sadly, the politicians did not reframe the problem in this light on this occasion, but did win the media round to stopping their support of a small minority of protesters.

Think of a serious business problem you are facing, See if you can find the real problem by reframing your apparent issue in more abstract terms.

The double loop

The ideas so far in this section are capable of standing on their own. However, the most powerful creative tool I know operates at a more strategic level and is able to revolutionize the creativity of an orga-nization. It is the idea of "double-loop thinking," as invented by Harvard professor Chris Argyris.

Single-loop thinking is problem solving by another name. If the photocopier breaks down, for example, someone fixes it.

Double-loop thinking seeks to step back from a single instance of failure and learn from it. It looks at underlying systems and behaviors and seeks to fix these. In the case of the broken photocopier, it would involve asking questions about whether the specification of the machine is appropriate, why photocopying is being done in-house, and whether a paper-less approach might be better. Double-loop thinking requires you to reflect on what you have learned and do things differently as a result.

Use this simple chart to work on some of your own business issues. I have included one example to get you going:

Issue or problem	Single-loop solution	Double-loop solution
Working too many hours	Spend less time with family Etc.	Be much clearer about priorities and do less business entertaining

Hothousing

You have probably heard the expression "a hothouse of ideas." It conjures up the image of a person or team brimming with creative concepts. But, what is it about a hothouse that could usefully be applied to the business situation?

Gardeners use hothouses for many things, including:

◆ Growing tender plants from seeds.
◆ Accelerating the growth of plants.
◆ As a test bed for new species.
◆ Controlling the environment of a particular plant.
◆ Protecting plants from the harsh climate outside.

You can see how all of these techniques transfer readily to the business environment. Good ideas need to be nurtured. However, what is less well known is what gardeners say to their plants while they are being nurtured. Even Prince Charles is said to talk to his favorite plants.

In a business, in contrast, what you say is essential. Sneering, for example, one of my seven serious sins on page 161, is a disastrous way to treat people. To create an effective hothousing environment, you need to develop a language that rewards the tentative, encourages the sharing of ideas, promotes hunches, values insights, and gives constructive feedback at appropriate moments.

Comments such as the following are obviously helpful:

"That sounds great."

"I am really excited to hear that."

"How could we try it out?"

"Let's explore how that would look."

What else can you think of? Make the longest list you possibly can. Then try the list activity out on a team of people you work with. Make a group list and create posters with some of the most powerful statements. You could also illustrate them.

Finding fun and funkiness at work

It was Carl Jung who said, "Without this playing with fantasy, no creative work has ever come to birth." Organizations ignore his wise remark at their peril. Eric Hoffer goes further: "The compulsion to take ourselves seriously is in inverse proportion to our creative capacity."

John Grant has always played with fantasy and tried not to take himself too seriously to get the best for his many clients. This is how he describes the story of how IKEA came to tell the British people to "chuck out your chintz" and even made the British Prime Minister smile!

Back in late 1995, I was a co-founder of a new ad agency called St Luke's. We had just set the company up and were pitching for our first new client—IKEA. We were about a week away from the final presentation and the pressure was mounting.

I went off one wet Wednesday evening to research some rough ideas about "How does IKEA manage to make such great furniture so cheap?" or something like that. This kind of research is called "focus groups." Although that's a bit of a misnomer because they are ideally quite defocused! That way you can hope to learn something new.

In the course of a series of these focus groups, I had come to realize that something was holding us back. Everybody quite liked the ads we were suggesting. (They were very funny.) But they didn't exactly seem to be about to change the world. Something was missing and I just couldn't quite put my finger on what.

Until on a dark February evening a man in one of these focus groups, in a suburb in Wembley, leant forward and said, "Yes, that's all very well but I wouldn't have that chair in my living room!"

"Why not?" I asked him.

"Because it's too modern."

That was it!

IKEA was the only big retailer selling modern furniture in the UK apart from Habitat which is also owned by IKEA. If significant numbers of people felt like the man in Wembley, then IKEA's plans to expand into Middle England would be thwarted. Conversely if we could shift the taste of the nation towards modern furniture then IKEA would benefit disproportionately.

That was the simple bit. The harder thing with any new idea is convincing the people around you and making something that actually works.

The convincing process started with the St Luke's team. A week from the pitch presentation this was all highly destabilizing. And as a strategy "changing people's tastes" was unconventional if not a little funky! How did we know taste was the main problem? How on earth could we shift something as deeply held as tastes with something as flimsy as advertising? And how could we convince a client we hardly knew, even if we could convince ourselves.

For a few days it was very touch and go. The team was split down the middle on this idea. But the strength of the St Luke's culture was an almost reckless disposition for backing people's hunches and ideas, even if it meant losing clients in the process. Then a telephone survey of 1,000 UK adults over the weekend gave us more confidence. Two-thirds said that their taste leaned towards traditional English styles. And two-thirds of those who didn't shop at IKEA said it was because the furniture was "too modern." Our man in Wembley turned out to be far more representative than we'd expected.

By the following Wednesday we had a rationale and the beginnings of an ad campaign aimed at changing the taste of a nation. To our surprise IKEA bought it (and us). That's typical IKEA. They make a point of daring to be different. And they liked St Luke's because we shared their values, which helped.

It still took us two or three more months of creative development to come up with the "Chuck Out Your Chintz" campaign. (Based on the idea of a modern version of "burn your bra"—furniture feminism.) It was aired in September that year. By December IKEA sales had doubled. By spring it was being quoted by politicians and newspapers as part of the New Britain mood—"Tony Blair tough on Chintz, Tough on the Causes of Chintz." And by 1999 a survey of UK adults' taste showed a complete swing; two-thirds now saying they liked modern styles.

Once upon a time, about five years ago, it was possible to say that only advertising, media, or entertainment companies, the Disneys of this world, needed to have a sense of fun. It was possible, but wrong. In today's business world, many people are actively seeking a sense of fun.

As increasing numbers of organizations are competing to deliver similar services, having a corporate sense of humor is increasingly important. So, for example, we see Richard Branson wearing a wedding dress in the pages of the British press to advertise Virgin Brides.

Or, after a dramatic attempt to steal a valuable diamond from the Millennium Dome in London involving undercover police officers and robbers driving a JCB digger truck, it was a clever move by JCB to run ads using the image of its product so surprisingly caught in the limelight!

The rapidly growing communications company ntl is another example. It has a vision statement about "making money, having some fun and doing some good."

This kind of combination of values and approaches to doing business is becoming much more common.

What ideas do you have that could make your work more fun? For a moment, think of the most outrageous suggestions you can and apply them to the way your organization:

- ◆ *promotes itself*
- ◆ *communicates with its staff*
- ◆ *deals with its customers*
- ◆ *organizes its meetings*

A WORLD OF POSSIBILITY

You learned, on page 46, about the idea of "learned optimism" as developed by Martin Seligman. I would like to take this concept one stage further and suggest that, to be truly smart, you need to understand the world of "learned possibility." Seligman's learned optimism concept is based on the way you interpret events as they happen to you. Mine is about a view of the future that is separated from the restrictions of optimism or pessimism. It is not about being half full or half empty, but about the possibility that you might be filled to the brim, that anything can be done.

It is a kind of mental modeling that I am convinced brings huge benefits.

Mike Leibling, director of Trainset, puts it like this: "If you have one idea, it's a compulsion. If you have two ideas, it's a dilemma. But if you have three or more ideas, then you have a choice."

Here are just a few practical suggestions as to how you can move into the world of possibility:

- Give yourself one goal only each day.
- Make time for at least one period of at least 20 minutes of total relaxation each day.
- Always look at problems from at least three points of view.
- Make a note every day of what surprises you.
- Try to surprise someone you work with every day.
- As well as writing them down, always visualize problems.
- Use all your senses.
- Use music somehow every day of your life.
- Make sure you become absorbed for an hour or more in at least one task every day.
- If you use brainstorming, focus on what you do in the last five minutes.
- Hold some meetings standing up.
- Send fewer group emails.
- Make a point of speaking in person to at least one person you were planning to email every day.

◆   Make sure someone visits another organization to learn from them every week of the year.
◆   Visit another organization yourself at least once a month.
◆   Ask "lay consultants" to work with you on some projects.
◆   Get your family to help you with a difficult work problem from time to time.
◆   Break established patterns from time to time.
◆   Take a 20-minute walk every day.
◆   Pay for staff to have a drink with each other once every month.
◆   Put the "s" back into Away Days: one day is not enough.
◆   Reinvent yourself at least once a year.
◆   Be happy to say that you will "sleep on it."

What three ideas do you have to ensure that you live in a world of possibility?

1

2

3

HARNESSING YOUR CREATIVITY—IN A NUTSHELL

YOU HAVE LEARNED:

✔ that creativity is a key element of learning to learn
✔ that your brain operates at different "speeds"
✔ that many people have their best ideas after a period of activity
✔ how to harness your creativity using as many of your intelligences as possible
✔ that there are some real barriers to creativity
✔ that you can make your workplace more likely to develop a multiple intelligence workforce
✔ that creativity involves making new connections

KEY IDEAS
State of flow
Brain waves
Multiple intelligence
Six hat thinking
Soft thinking
Double-loop thinking

KEY TECHNIQUES/
APPROACHES
Using dialog
Moving outside your field
Association games
Lateral thinking
Problem finding
Hothousing
Having fun at work

10

The Case for Learning at Work

W HEN PRICE WAS THE KEY DETERMINANT OF SUCCESS, WE NEEDED TO focus on ways of keeping prices down. When the nature of the product was most important, product development and quality assurance were where we put much of our effort. So, why are more and more people showing an interest in the minds of their employees? Why is learning becoming more important in the new economy? It must surely be because of a renewed interest in people.

Listen to what these business leaders have to say. Colin Marshall, chairman of British Airways, argues:

Learning is extremely important as a vital raw material, but it is the inventive application which creates the true competitive resource. Continuous learning at all levels and across all functions is the life blood of truly innovative companies. The more we know about ourselves, about our markets and about the way we do things, the more we can deliver to all stakeholders—customers, shareholders and employees—alike.

Sir Bob Reid is adamant:

You have to be at the top of the learning curve to be successful, offering imaginative products which meet customers' needs.

Sir Michael Bichard is passionate in his beliefs:

Learning is central to competitiveness. We must invest in high-quality learning for all our people and do something about our serious adult basic skill needs.

A number of leaders emphasize the context of rapid change. Chris Mellor at Anglian Water puts it like this:

You need bright flexible minds in a world of change. We haven't realized more than a fifth of our potential. Give a person the right environment and they can learn and soar.

Joyce Taylor is even more specific:

Learning has to be linked to business strategy. It matters to us because the sector is changing so fast. Learning is about flexibility, having minds which cope well with this sort of fast-moving environment. Employees have to learn to have open minds.

For companies whose business is the delivery of services, like Virgin One Account, learning is really important. As Jayne-Anne Gadhia says:

Flexibility is going to be hugely important as we have more service-led organizations. Workforces need to be as adaptable and empathetic as possible. This is what matters.

The same is true for an organization such as the FI Group. Hilary Cropper explains: "Learning is essential for a business like ours which is all about relationships."

Zoe van Zwanenberg, chief executive of the Scottish Leadership Foundation, makes it clear that there is just as powerful a case in the public sector:

Learning is critical. If public services are to be of value, then we have to learn to respond to wants and needs.

The leaders I interviewed had the learning of themselves and their people high up their organizational agenda.

Six reasons it pays to learn

There is, in fact, a robust, six-point business case for learning. It has six connected elements. Interestingly, the case is the same for both organizations and individuals although, obviously, the language you might express it in would be different.

1   *Performance*. You can increase productivity and improve quality through learning, becoming faster and better. This applies equally in a business and a personal context.

2   *Being better than your rivals*. In an age where human capital is all important, learning may well be the only sustainable source of competitive advantage, just as in the last two centuries buildings and financial capital were critical. For a dot-com or a communications company this is easy to see. But, even in more conventional manufacturing businesses, where knowledge of customer databases is important, it is not difficult to see the importance of better information. For an individual, it has always been the case that learning, whether in the shape of qualifications or not, gives you the edge at work.

3   *Knowledge as one of the outcomes of learning*. As US academic Warren Bennis puts it: "The major challenge for leaders in the twenty-first century will be how to release the brainpower of their organizations." In practice, this involves understanding that many of the things that individuals and organizations know remain at a tacit or implicit level too often. If they are going to be of any use, they have to become explicit and then be shared. So, for example, a team that has just completed a very demanding project will have gained competences in a range of areas, which, unless they are described and shared, will be of no use to the rest of the business. Or, at an individual level, you probably do not stop to think about how you drive a car until you have to help a son or daughter learn. Then you need to be able to explain your knowledge explicitly to be helpful in the passenger seat.

There are at least three myths about knowledge management: that it is a new phenomenon, that it is mainly about computer systems, and that knowledge can be managed at all. Knowledge can only be acquired through learning. Something is understood and an insight is acquired. That insight is then shared. In this process, people are the key and the speed and effectiveness of their learning are the determinants of success.

4   *Change.* In the twentieth century there were predictable cycles of innovation lasting several years. More than two decades ago, UK management guru Reg Revans taught that unless a company's learning is faster than the speed of external change, it will not thrive. Accelerated learning is essential for survival, bringing flexibility and adaptability. Businesses need multiskilled employees, with the lifelong learner adding most value. Rapid learning is required just to survive. This applies in your private life too. How effectively you deal with an unexpected house move, with divorce, or with the loss of a parent or family member will be largely determined by how adaptable you have learned to become.

5   *Learning is the key to successful cultural change.* Too often, people are simply told to do something differently. However, if you engage people in a dialog about how to do things differently and let them learn new ways for themselves, they will become involved and cultures will change.

6   *Learning is a great motivator.* When employability is the key to people retaining their jobs, they naturally want to improve their skills. The Campaign for Learning showed in a 1998 MORI poll that 77 percent of employees would prefer to work for an employer that supported their learning than one that gave them an increase in salary. Individuals who have, in their own time, taken courses or engaged in learning activities in their local community know just how positive such experiences can be and how much this can motivate them.

Learning pays, then, for organizations and for individuals. Indeed, in recognition of this fact, the British government launched a new financial product called an Individual Learning Account (ILA). The essential idea is that people should start to invest in their own learning in the same way that they currently invest in their house, their health, or their future pension. Under this scheme, a kind of new-economy virtual savings bond, individuals can claim tax rebates of up to 80 percent on the cost of learning. The discount is given at the point of sale and can be as much as £400 per annum. Long term, the idea could be for the ILA to be the means by which people might pay for all their learning throughout their lives. It would become the method of saving for learning and the account could also receive investments from third parties such as an employer, or, if opened at birth, from a grandparent, for example.

A world in which learning was normal, paid for just as we pay for the other important things in our lives, would doubtless be a better place. Indeed, learning can become almost addictive, and it is important to remind yourself that, to quote Warren Bennis again, "You can learn anything you want to learn."

THE CASE FOR LEARNING AT WORK—IN A NUTSHELL

YOU HAVE LEARNED:

✔ that many of today's organizations are already making the connection between learning and success
✔ that there is a strong business case for learning
✔ six good reasons that learning pays

KEY IDEAS
L > C
Individual Learning
Accounts

Part III

Steady As You Go

Putting learning into practice

PART III LOOKS LIKE THIS

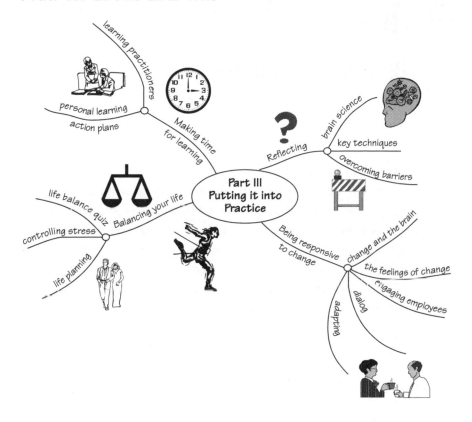

A KEY SENTENCE TO REMEMBER FROM THIS PART

The human species is what it is only because of its capacity to learn, reflect on that learning, adapt to it, and change. Over a long period of time our brain has grown in size and complexity.

A FAMOUS THOUGHT TO CONSIDER

We must be the change we wish to see in the world.

Mahatma Gandhi

11

Living and Learning

Ready, Go, and now Steady.

I have argued so far that, to power up your mind, you need to get yourself ready to learn. Now, I want to try to persuade you that, however competent you are as a learner, you will not learn faster and work smarter unless you really put your learning into practice, reflecting, changing, and adapting as you do so. Learning is not a spectator sport. The fourth and fifth of my 5Rs, Reflectiveness and Responsiveness, are at the heart of this capacity to thrive and develop.

PUTTING LEARNING INTO ACTION

As Charles Darwin wrote in *On the Origin of Species*:

It is not the strongest of the species that survive, nor the most intelligent, but the ones most responsive to change.

Biologically speaking, the human species is what it is only because of its capacity to learn, reflect on that learning, adapt to it, and change. Over a long period, our brain has grown in size and complexity. Over an equally long period, we lost our tail so that we now have a tiny stump at the base of our spine, and we moved from all fours to the two-legged creatures we are today.

The development of language was also probably a gradual process, moving from gestures through grunts to the articulation of words. Sometimes things happened suddenly, however. There must have been one day when we suddenly learned how to make fire, for example. In some cases, interestingly, we are still evolving. Take our appendix. Unless we have had it removed, it remains in our bodies as a throwback to the days when we were grass eaters.

Adaptation in animals obviously happens unconsciously, as in the example of the blue tits and robins on page 109. But, think about the robins and blue tits as if they were people for a moment. If you were a robin and able to reflect on what was happening to you, you might have wanted to talk about why you no longer seemed to be able to get to the cream on the top of milk bottles. You might have begun to notice that the tops were being pecked open and that there often seemed to be a small bird leaving a bottle every time you approached it.

You might even have put all your territorial instincts aside for a day and called all the robins in an area together to share what they knew about the mystery of the bottle top.

In the early days of the internet when Microsoft was doubtful about its likely impact, this is what Bill Gates famously did, calling on all staff to reflect on the situation and, almost overnight, changing the company's view of the serious business opportunity presented by the World Wide Web.

As Jayne-Anne Gadhia puts it: "The most important consequence of learning is new behavior."

Who would have predicted, for example, that we would come to rely so much on computers and that our lifestyle would become so sedentary?

The evolution of humans has taken many thousands of years. Naturally, your own personal evolution has and will take place over a much shorter timescale. You will probably already have experienced key moments, similar in their impact on you to the discovery of fire for humanity. Obvious examples of this would include the birth of a child, the loss of a family member, going through a divorce, or obtaining a new job.

Apart from our ability to use fire, what do you think the main steps have been in humanity's evolution?

> Use the idea of evolution to reflect on your own life so far. What have been the most power-
> ful moments to date?
> What have you learned from these? Which kind of experiences have shaped your development
> most so far? (This is an interesting activity to undertake with other colleagues at work and
> with your partner at home.)
> What are the biggest changes you are facing at work and at home? How responsive are you
> to these changes?

CHANGE AND THE BRAIN

You have seen how the human brain has evolved "upwards" from its most primitive reptilian form, capable of little more than fight or flight responses. As it has been required to undertake more complex tasks, so it has grown in complexity and size. As evolutionary biologists have made clear, it has changed in complexity and size over thousands of years. All change involves some stress, but if stress levels become too high, the brain ceases to operate as effectively as it should. This can often be because the people engaged in the change feel that they have lost control of their lives.

You have read various theories of how we learn. It was Jean Piaget who wrote of learning by assimilation and by accommodation. You assimilate bits and pieces through reading books and watching a television program. You accommodate through experience by reflecting on what you have been through and changing your behavior accordingly. David Kolb's theory of the learning cycle also is helpful. You establish a concept, test it, experience it, and reflect on the experience. As a result, you do things differently.

You have explored some of the theories of motivation and may remember the discussion about intrinsic and external motivation. All the recent research has shown that people perform best when they are intrinsically motivated, unless they are involved with very mechanistic tasks. People who are engaged in solving a problem and who are involved in finding the solution to it "own" that solution. Put simply, we feel patronized if we are simply told to change, even if we are offered attractive rewards. The human mind wants to evolve its own solution and create its own new paradigm.

We need to reflect on what we have experienced and draw any necessary conclusions from it.

Finally, the brain is a very sophisticated survival mechanism. It ensures that the right chemicals are produced when it needs to stimulate the body to run away from danger. It knows how to recognize bodily and facial danger signals from other people and other creatures. To ensure its survival, the brain is incredibly flexible, or plastic, as neuroscientists prefer to say. Even if it is severely damaged—for example, through disease or as the result of a stroke—it can adapt. Parts of the brain not normally used for one function can take on that role.

There is, in short, plenty of reserve capacity in the brain. But, to be truly effective you need to learn how to analyze what has happened and take action accordingly.

Interestingly, it is worth remembering that many of us succumb to "change blindness," seeing far less than we think we do. We take in only the important details of what happens and miss much of the rest.

Harvard scientists undertook a fascinating experiment. On a university campus, a researcher stopped an unsuspecting student to ask for some directions. As the student answered, two more researchers, carrying a door, passed between the student and the researcher asking the way. As they did so, a switch took place and a different researcher took the place of the original one. The conversation continued.

Once they had finished talking, the researcher asked the student if they had noticed anything: 50 percent of students had not! When your attention is fixed on one thing, your brain may not notice other details.

Have you ever experienced change blindness? Can you think of any applications at work? At home?

LIVING AND LEARNING—IN A NUTSHELL

YOU HAVE LEARNED:

✔ that reflection is essential if our learning is to be effective
✔ that responsiveness, the capacity to change and adapt, is a key element of learning to learn
✔ some more brain science to deepen your understanding of change

KEY IDEA
Change blindness

12

Reflectiveness

The purpose of playing, whose end, both at the first and now, was and is, to hold, as 'twere, the mirror up to nature.

William Shakespeare, *Hamlet*

HOW OFTEN DO FIND YOURSELF RETURNING FROM A TRAINING COURSE full of great new ideas but, within hours of being back at work, forgetting the insights you had gained? Or, consistently failing to apply the lessons you learned from a new product launch or a meeting with a client? Or, perhaps something goes quite badly wrong and you don't want to spend any more time on it, preferring instead to move on and, in the process, sweeping it under the carpet?

Do you ever find yourself feeling uneasy about an event of which you are part and not quite sure why this is? Do you ever get into a state of uncertainty, not sure with which of a number of perfectly reasonable courses of action you should proceed?

Do things happen to you at work and leave you with a sneaking suspicion that the problem is not at work but in your private life?

One of the facts of modern living is that we spend a great deal of time thinking about our external image: the clothes we wear, the car we drive, the house we live in, or the places we choose to go to eat. The media act as mirrors, continually telling us what kind of person selects a particular brand. If we choose to deconstruct these media mirrors, we can get a picture of ourselves from the outside as a consumer.

The kind of mirror we really need is the one that tells us something about the person beneath the image and how they are doing, as Hamlet was able to find out about the real Claudius with the help of the players. This has always been difficult but, arguably, it is even more difficult today, for two reasons.

The first is image consciousness itself. There is a sense in which you can get yourself into a situation where you have so effectively defined yourself as the kind of successful person who simply bounces back from anything that goes wrong, that you leave yourself no time to reflect on things when they do not go according to plan. You just drag yourself out of bed the following morning and carry on as if nothing has happened.

The second reason is that today's business environment is so pressured that many people feel their promotion prospects or their job itself will be at risk if, in the process of reflecting, they admit to making mistakes. It is always difficult to own up to making a mistake at work, or at home for that matter—but the benefits of doing so are enormous to the individual and to the organization.

Sometimes, of course, you do not realize the effect of what you are doing. Over time you have acquired certain behaviors that are seen by those around you as unhelpful. Perhaps you have become so used to your position of authority that you make unreasonable demands on other people. Or, perhaps you interfere too much in the decision-making process, effectively disempowering those who work with you. In such cases, you sometimes need someone else to hold a mirror up to you so you can see yourself as others see you, but without losing your self-respect along the way.

The truth is that unless you reflect on what you have learned and then go and do something differently, your learning is going to be of only limited value. While the skill of reflecting is a difficult one to acquire, it is also one of the most beneficial. Getting into reflective habits will be key to your success.

How reflective are you at work? At home? When do you reflect? How do you make sure you build in time for reflection?

Reflectiveness is connected to the passage of time—by definition, it involves looking back at what has happened. However, effective reflection also involves taking stock of the present and thinking forward to the future. You don't reflect simply for the sake of it, useful as the thought process is. You reflect on something in order to learn from it and do it differently when you are in a similar situation again.

THE SCIENCE OF REFLECTING

I have already touched on some of the science behind this area. You have seen how the brain responds well to challenge and how it needs to process or reflect on this. You experience something and the brain attempts to fit it into existing patterns, to classify it, in effect to reflect on it. If the brain receives a painful stimulus when you bump into something, it remembers this and you work out a different route in future. This is how the mind operates.

Nevertheless, there are some aspects of the way in which the brain works that can deter you from reflecting on your mistakes. So, for example, the negative effect of stress on the mind means that it can be very difficult to work in places where reflection and admission of failure are not possible. Worries build up and performance levels go down.

The brain's instinctive pattern making also produces another tendency that can be negative as well as positive: making connections and filling in gaps. This is why you see things that are not in fact present in some visual puzzles. Your brain completes the picture, filling in the gaps. The same operates in the workplace. A mistake is made and your brain begins to worry away at what happened. If the culture of the organization is one in which it is not acceptable to admit to mistakes, there will be an uneasy vacuum after any major error. Gossip and rumor will move in to try to provide a solution. And workplace gossip may be much more unhelpful than the plain admission of fault, reflection on why it happened, and a decision to move on better prepared in the future.

Because your brain is a pattern-making mechanism, it has often done its reflection without your being consciously aware of it. So, you may be able to wake up the morning after something has happened with a clearer sense of its meaning.

And finally, if your brain does not get feedback, it cannot know whether what it has experienced is something you want it to have more of or not, if it is important or trivial, life enhancing or life threatening.

THE CRAFT OF REFLECTING

As Mike Hughes has written: "Trying to learn without reviewing is like trying to fill a bath without putting the plug in."

Unless you are prepared to make a real effort to review and reflect on what you have experienced, your learning—just like the bath water—is being wasted. The more you can learn from what you have done, the more you will be able to adapt and change.

Many people choose to write down their reflections. Here are three different approaches.

Will Hutton, ex-Fleet Street editor, not surprisingly chooses the medium of the printed page:

I am a writer. I have to express myself on paper. The act of writing forces me to sort out what I think. It's like storytelling. The same is true of public speaking. I trust my brain to come up with what I think and what I want to say.

In an echo of this, Sir Michael Bichard says:

Learning is about reflecting on experience and situations, working out how to do things differently. I do a lot of public speaking and use these oppor-tunities as a chance to force myself to reflect on what has gone before.

Sir Bob Reid is quite specific:

In all my jobs I meticulously write down what I feel about things in the first weeks. Then I put it away for six months and look at it again later to reflect on what I wrote and felt.

Zoe van Zwanenberg keeps an occasional journal:

At certain times of the year, I take quiet time and think through what I have seen. Then I let my mind wander around the parallels and meanings. I often work by association.

There are two main aspects to the skill of reflecting: thinking about your experiences, and thinking about the process of your learning.

Looking back and learning from experiences

Effective reflection requires you to be open and exploratory. It is also important not to be defensive and not to take things personally.

There is a tendency not to bother to reflect on the things that go well, because you are happy and already mentally moving on to your next project. The same is true with regard to things that go badly. For different reasons, you want to move on, to forget all that happened, it fact to pretend it never happened.

It is slightly more common to take stock of challenging assignments that you manage to complete. Something in the nature of these, like a difficult walk up a mountain when you nearly get lost in thick fog, induces camaraderie and sharing. It seems natural and part of bonding to share your thoughts and feelings when you have survived, just as it does back in the pub after an adventure on a mountain.

What about you? Which kind of experiences do you find it easiest to reflect on: the ones that have gone well, the ones that really challenged you, or the ones that went wrong in some way? You may want to try keeping a learning log to explore your own experiences.

Later in this chapter there are some specific suggestions as to how you might like to reflect on experiences and how you can overcome the barriers to reflection that exist in most workplaces.

Looking back on how you learned something

In the context of learning to learn, it is your capacity to reflect on how you went about learning something that you will find particularly useful. If you are going to develop new techniques, you need to review their effectiveness and check how they work for you.

Ideally, you need to reflect at two levels: on an ongoing basis and after each learning experience. As I have stressed already, how you reflect is very much a matter of personal style and taste.

Study the list of skills below. They are the ones at the heart of your intelligence. How confident are you about doing them?

Description	Very confident	Confident	Need to practice
Identifying how much of your learning is solitary and how much collaborative			
Choosing to learn online			
Using media or books about learning			
Planning to use a particular medium and then trying it out			
Consciously modeling or imitating others			
Distinguishing between formal and informal learning experiences			
Keeping a written record of your learning			
Practicing or strengthening under-utilized styles			
Identifying how much of your learning is passive versus active			
Finding out how other people learn			
Breaking learning into a series of "hows"			

Description	Very confident	Confident	Need to practice
Constantly seeking to add new learning techniques to your repertoire from all possible sources			
Identifying how much of your learning is absorbing facts or information versus experiences or trial and error			
Persisting with new learning methods or techniques until they become easier			
Habitually exploring how you learn			
Pondering the different feelings, pleasant and unpleasant, triggered by different learning experiences			
Focusing on developing your preferred learning style(s)			
Experimenting, on a trial-and-error basis, with different ways of learning			
Deliberately choosing challenging learning options			
Using mind maps or spider diagrams			
Consciously using a learning model, for example, the learning cycle or the idea of multiple intelligences			
Pondering your original motives for learning and those that keep you going			

Description	Very confident	Confident	Need to practice
Using techniques to activate your memory			
Using a variety of study skills or techniques			
Understanding the different roles played by people when learning together			
Getting in touch with the feelings or emotions that suffuse learning			
Answering the question, "How can I improve the way that I learn?"			
Learning from people who do it differently			
Accepting accidental, unplanned experiences and working out how they contribute to your learning			
Undertaking activities to strengthen learning skills and/or overcome weaknesses			

When it comes to reflecting on the daily experiences of your life, you obviously will not want to be considering a long list of items. Indeed, if you want to become a regular reflector, you need to find simple formulae and templates that you can apply, like what went well and why, what went badly and why.

Think of something that has gone really badly for you recently. Apply the formula above to it. Let your mind wander, as Zoe van Zwanenberg suggests, gently looking for connections, parallels, and associations. Include this in a learning log for a period of time.

MAKING REFLECTION NORMAL

For many people, it is a crisis in their lives that forces them to take stock, often through such things as divorce, redundancy, ill health, or the death of a loved one.

There are less traumatic ways of doing it!

When do you stop and reflect? Look back over your last week. How many minutes have you spent reflecting on things that have happened to you or the way you have learned something? Use the chart below to help you.

Topic	Minutes spent	When

Most people find it helpful to set aside a regular time every day—it need only be a few minutes. The beginning of the day is a good time. Some favor lunchtime reflection, especially if you can get out of your working environment. And, for many people who travel for long distances to work, the journey home can be useful. The act of reflection normally calms you down, which is a good thing in itself before you return home—unless, that is, you are reflecting on really stressful issues!

5 simple things you can do at work to reflect more

1   Ensure that all team meetings start with a brief feedback session to learn from what has gone before.
2   Create feedback and reflection templates to accompany every aspect of your work and make them available in paper and electronic format.
3   Have separate sections of all noticeboards for reflective comments.
4   Have a dedicated section of your intranet devoted to reflection and evaluation.
5   Make 360 degree feedback (feedback from all those who work with and for you as part of a performance process) commonplace, with everyone invited to be part of an appraisal scheme, not just your superior.

Of course, the more you model behavior that encourages reflection, the more likely those around you will be to see its value.

OVERCOMING THE BARRIERS TO REFLECTING

The main enemy of reflection is, of course, the relentless pressure of time. I just have not got time to stop and reflect, we say to ourselves in offices across the world. But there is also a deeply rooted cultural tendency in many of us to assume that experts know best and that our opinion cannot possibly be of value. This habit of mind is acquired by some at school, when the realization dawns that in many examinations there are right and wrong answers regardless of the validity of the question!

Another aspect of this is the fear of failure. Colin Marshall here honestly describes a failure from which he has learned:

Somebody once said that mistakes are not worth making if you cannot learn from them. Contorted logic it may be, but it is also common sense. Good recovery from mistakes says as much about an individual's or a company's competence or character as getting it right first time, in many ways more so. At British Airways, for example, we believed the British public wanted to accept us as a world airline, with world images as our symbols. We were wrong and set about listening closely to what our customers and the public at large were asking of us. The image has accordingly been very successfully adjusted and we have re-established a valuable, productive relationship with our customers.

It is refreshing to read such sentiments. All too often we hide behind experts. Shunryu Suzuki summarizes this attitude by saying: "In the beginner's mind there are many possibilities, but in the expert's there are few." It is a sad fact of increased competence that it seems to make people less willing to consider other possibilities or alternatives. It is, therefore, even more important to ensure that as you become more technically skilled in anything, you keep your mind open to feedback from others and evaluation from yourself.

Here are some other barriers to reflecting. How would you overcome them? What other barriers would you add?

Barrier	Means of overcoming it
It's difficult to admit to making mistakes	
You may get into trouble if you admit your mistakes	
It's easier not to start a line of thinking that may lead to changes	
Reflection is not real work	
There is nowhere to reflect quietly	
It's hard work thinking about why things work and don't work	

One of the subtle ways in which feedback can sometimes seem to be a burden is because of the word "back." Busy people find it psychologically difficult to allocate time to looking at what has already happened, but are much more ready to invest their efforts in the future. (Of course, feedback is designed to help you avoid the mistakes of the past as you move forward, but it does not always feel like that to some.)

Mike Leibling, director of Trainset, has created a good way of overcoming this barrier. He calls it *feedforward*. It is an excellent technique for reflecting in a group and it has very powerful and immediate outcomes.

This how it works. Each person first identifies a problem, something they would like to learn to do more effectively. The person with the problem becomes the client and articulates the brief for their problem.

Here is an example from my own experience. An experienced speaker tells the group that he wants to include jokes in his presentations, but can never remember the punchline or the story if it is a complex joke. He asks for help.

Members of the group take it in turns to offer him advice, starting with "Maybe..." or "Perhaps..." The individual is only allowed to say "Thank you" after each suggestion when about two minutes have gone by. Advice might include:

- Maybe you could write it down.
- Perhaps you could have a mental rehearsal of the joke.
- Maybe you could imagine the joke as a series of images so you were clearer about its structure.
- Perhaps you could slow your delivery down.
- Maybe you could use cartoons instead.
- Perhaps you could try looking at people in your audience more directly rather than looking up in the air as you struggle to remember the joke.

As you may have guessed, the person asking for advice in this case was me. I was offered many more suggestions than the ones I have listed here, but the last one on the list has turned out to be just what I needed.

In this example, I was able to be very specific about my need. But it might be that you want to be more general in framing the "brief" you give as the client.

Think of an area of your own life or learning that you would like help with and try this technique out with a group of colleagues or friends.

A REFLECTIVE WORLD

When Samuel Beckett said, "No matter. Try again. Fail again. Fail better," he was articulating an unusual view of the world. He seems almost to be glorying in failure. Perhaps Beckett had intuitively anticipated the NLP principle that there is no such thing as failure, only feedback.

Many people find writing a useful way of reflecting. Diary, journal, and log are all words that have come into our language from other spheres. The captain of a ship, for example, keeps a log, because without it, their vessel would have no record of its route or of the conditions that led to certain decisions being taken. The world in general seems to be divided into those who like to keep diaries and those who do not.

There is no doubt that the act of writing is itself mysterious, powerful and creative. You have already seen that in Will Hutton's words on page 198. Chris Mellor uses Anglian Water's intranet to write an occasional reflective column on what he has learned over a period of a few weeks. Many people find the journal format a satisfying one.

But, all modes of communication—writing, speaking, listening, and reading—have important roles to play in the process of reflection.

Look at this list of different approaches. How many of these have you tried? Which do you prefer?

Keeping a diary.

Writing letters to yourself.

Making up newspaper headlines that encapsulate how well you feel something went.

Using unfinished sentences like "The best thing about...," "The thing I remember most is...," "That made me feel that..."

Using sentences that involve all your senses: "I saw the...," "I heard that...," "When I touched the...," etc.

Using a mind map to capture your thoughts.

Using free-noting techniques.

Using pre-formatted templates with questions.

Writing down your feelings as events happen and keeping a note of the time.

Telling your own version as a story.

Talking about good and bad moments.
Making a short "How did it go?" telephone call.
Talking to a colleague about an experience.
Listening to feedback from another colleague.
Being coached on aspects of your performance or learning.
Reading reports from other colleagues.
Quietly reflecting on your own.

You might like to try meditation. There are many different approaches to this, but they all tend to involve establishing a successful routine for reflecting at a deep level. This often includes the selection of a quiet, secure environment, closing your eyes, deliberate breathing, concentrated attention on a mantra or the sound of your own breathing in an attempt to clear the mind of its clutter, and the achievement of a slower brain rhythm, the alpha state that we have already explored.

Franz Kafka writes in his *Reflections*:

You do not have to leave your room. Remain sitting at your table and listen. Do not even listen, simply wait. The world will freely offer itself to you to be unmasked, it has no choice, it will roll in ecstasy at your feet.

These are exciting thoughts!

The benefits of meditation are well documented. They include:

◆   Reduced stress.
◆   A refreshed state of mind.
◆   A more positive frame of mind.
◆   Better health.
◆   Better sleeping.
◆   Greater alertness.
◆   Increased happiness.

REFLECTIVENESS—IN A NUTSHELL

YOU HAVE LEARNED:

✔ about the brain science behind reflectiveness
✔ that there are two aspects to reflecting: learning from experience and learning how you went about learning
✔ about some of the barriers to reflecting and how you can overcome them
✔ some techniques for reflecting

KEY IDEAS
Feedforward
Feedback not failure

KEY TECHNIQUES/
APPROACHES
Keeping a learning log
Setting time aside each day for reflecting
Building reflecting into different processes at work
Meditation

13

Responsiveness

I T HAS ALWAYS BEEN NECESSARY TO BE RESPONSIVE TO CHANGE AND PEOPLE
have always reacted to the prospect of change differently—some
resisting it, some welcoming it. Responsiveness and the capacity to
react intelligently to change go hand in hand with the ability to be
successful. As Hilary Cropper puts it:

*Change is endemic. Organizations and individuals need to be able to
change their spots, to live with some discomfort. It's all about survival.*

According to Thomas Huhn, change tends to be articulated both by
younger people and by those who are new to the area of work. Writing
some 30 years ago, Huhn is credited with being the inventor of the
word "paradigm" in his fascinating book *The Structure of Scientific
Revolutions*. As we watch the impact of technology on the business
environment today, Huhn's observations seem strangely prescient.

A paradigm is a framework or pattern, a way of making sense of
the world. Moore's law, the idea that computer power doubles every
18 months, is an example of a paradigm. So is the now discredited
notion that you can have a job for life in one organization or sector.

Most change is comparatively gradual in the great scheme of
things. Even if you feel that the change you are anticipating is enormous—a paradigm shift—it will be helpful to show how it can be
achieved by a series of incremental moves. These will be easier for
the minds of the people involved to grasp. Most people would prefer to have some kind of model for what they are being asked to do.

From the perspective of the mind, there are a number of principles that those managing change may want to consider:

- Build on the past.
- Inform people fully, dealing honestly with difficult issues.
- Engage people in creating the solution.
- Provide a clear alternative vision.
- Create a culture of support.
- Minimize uncertainty.
- Once you have decided what you are doing, do it quickly.

Most of these will be self-explanatory from what you know already about how the brain works. The last one is particularly important, as it is sometimes wrongly thought that a long-drawn-out approach is kinder to those involved; in reality, that is more likely to lead to stress and uncertainty.

Chris Mellor of Anglian Water is convinced about the need to involve employees. As he says: "With major change people always assume the worst. It is essential that you get people emotionally involved or you will not get their commitment."

Think back to a significant change you have recently experienced at work, one that has happened to you rather than one you have led. Apply these principles to it, using the chart below.

Questions to consider	How was this principle acknowledged?	How did you feel?	How could the principle have been more effectively built into the process of change?
Build on the past			
Inform people fully, dealing honestly with difficult issues			
Engage people in creating the solution			
Provide a clear alternative vision			
Create a culture of support			
Minimize uncertainty			
Once you have decided what you are doing, do it quickly			

THE FEELINGS OF CHANGE

Sometimes, change is thrust on us as a result of external factors.
You lose your job. Someone close to you dies. You become unwell.
For a while, you feel that things are out of your control—and there
is a real sense in which they are.

You may also decide to do things differently because you
have learned that there is a better way. You have overcome your
anxiety about public speaking and now actively seek to gain experiences. Or, you realize that you have become unreasonably defensive in your dealings with a certain colleague and resolve to adopt a
more open and accepting style of behaving.

In many situations, even if at first it appears that things are
beyond your influence, they are not. Not many external situations
appear totally out of the blue: you see them coming if you are prepared to look. As an effective learner, it is essential that you can
learn to do things differently. Being able to move from learning
through reflection to deciding to change is a key element of using
your intelligence. A major element of this is learning to anticipate
and manage your feelings.

In almost all experiences of change, the feelings you have follow a pattern, especially when the change you are contemplating
has been largely instigated, in your view, by external factors. Here
is a typical cycle of the feelings associated with change:

Of course, it is not always like this or in this order. And often, you will enter as a willing pioneer and your emotions will be largely or wholly positive.

Understanding the kind of emotions you may encounter may help you to deal with change more effectively. Suppose, for example, you have learned that the reason your good senior staff regularly leave the business is because you never give them a chance to be creative. You have decided to do something about this, to change your ways and ensure that you actively seek to release the creativity of those around you. It may help you to be prepared for moments of continuing denial as you move forward! Being prepared means that you can have a strategy in place to deal with the feelings that you have: "It's common to go though these kind of feelings, I'll just stay calm," for example.

Understanding the cycle of change also means that you will recognize the different responses you may have. British academic and author Amin Rajan, chief executive of Create, imagines what it would be like if you described the ways people react to change as if they were different kinds of soldiers.

So, at the most enthusiastic end of the scale he has "crusaders," people who are visionaries and pioneers, while at the other end he imagines "deserters," the staff who decide they have to leave and find another place to work.

The chart overleaf, developed from Amin's ideas, shows some different kinds of approaches to change, as exemplified by different soldiers. Much of it has been left blank for you to use. You may find it amusing to think about people you know well and assign them to the different categories!

When looking at charts like this, it is easy to smile and consign other people to one or more of these "types," secure in the knowledge that you are not like that.

But what about you? What roles do you play? What kind of soldier are you when it comes to change? Does your answer depend on how much you are in control of the change process?

	Beliefs and feelings	**Role and comments**
Crusader		Crusaders are believers, early pioneers. People who can say what they believe clearly and with conviction are invaluable.
Sapper		
Bandit		
Guerilla	It will all go away. I'll hide in the mountains. I can get away with it.	
General		
Army doctor		
Secret agent		
Liberator		
Collaborator		
Military police		
Conscientious objector		
Deserter		

RESPONDING TO CHANGE

How do *you* put the principles outlined on page 211 into practice? Or, more explicitly, how do you change the hearts and minds of all the employees in a large company, building on its past successes, involving and engaging people fully, providing a clear vision and creating a supportive culture, all undertaken at accelerated speed?

One company, ICL, has put much of this philosophy into practice with the help of the learning consultancy Celemi. Here is what happened.

When Keith Todd became Chief Executive of ICL in 1995, he joined a company that successfully made computers. Over the next few years, it became clear to him and his team that the future of the business lay in providing ebusiness services and not manufacturing computers. In early 1998, he began investing heavily in the 500 most senior people, to ensure that they had engaged, understood, and agreed with the transformation that was being envisaged.

However, ICL realized that unless all the workforce—22,000 employees—had an opportunity to study the information previously only available to the top people, learn from it, and decide to change, the process would be a slow and wasteful one. ICL might lose the very market advantage it was determined to secure.

Enter Elizabeth Lank, programme director for mobilizing knowledge at ICL and author of *The Power of Learning*. Elizabeth engaged Ian Windle, managing director of Celemi, to work with ICL to develop an imaginative way of really involving all its employees in the planned changes. The Conversations for Change initiative was born.

The chosen communication tool was WorkMats™. These are large, table-sized posters that form the basis for dialog between small groups of people. A number of design principles were agreed: that the process should engage people as individuals; that the same basic global conversation would be had in five different languages; that employees would want to take actions as a result of what they had learned; and, finally, that it would be a two-way process, giving management the chance to listen and adapt their plans.

The WorkMats focused on a number of issues:

◆   Where the company had come from, its rich and varied history.
◆   A chance to look at the future and see how it might affect individual lives in 2010.
◆   A look at how customers and press might view the 2010 vision.
◆   An examination of ICL's potential role in making the futures happen.
◆   An exploration of ICL's vision, strategy, and goals as developed by the management team.

A learning guide was produced for all participants and a WorkMat was specifically designed to facilitate and support conversations after the event about the actions that teams would be agreeing.

A 15-member team was assembled from all over the world and drawn from different business units. It was tasked with offering every employee the chance to take part in a small group dialog over a 12-week period. Two hundred ICL volunteers were trained as facilitators.

Conversations for Change was then run, using one facilitator for each group of about 24 employees. Using the Café VIK area of the company's intranet, employees booked a place at the most convenient location. As sessions began, feedback from them was also posted on the intranet as it was received. Most sessions were whole-day affairs, with special arrangements made to tailor them to the specific needs of certain employees working flexible hours, for example, in call centers.

To ensure that people really had the opportunity to engage their minds in this important piece of organizational and individual learning, each employee received a personal email inviting them to attend, followed up by a poster campaign in ICL building throughout the globe and on the intranet.

Not surprisingly, employees were initially skeptical about the degree to which this was a communication exercise, however imaginative, or about consultation and engagement. But, as the management group began to publish its responses to suggestions, clearly heeding employee advice, it soon became clear that the program was genuine in its intentions.

18,000 employees chose to attend the Conversations for Change, an impressive total by any reckoning. It proved that if you give people the big picture in a mind-friendly way, you are much more likely to get their active engagement.

However, as Elizabeth Lank put it: "The program has set a new expectation level for the company's investment in dialog with employees, and the company's leaders will need to meet—or exceed—that expectation in the years to come." A good challenge for any organization to have as an outcome of successfully releasing the natural intelligence of its employees!

Think about any significant period of change you have been through in an organization. Go through the story of it in your head or with a close friend or colleague. Reflect on any similarities to and differences from the ICL and Celemi example. What do you learn from this? Look at some examples of the different statements people make when faced with a challenging situation that is going to call on them to change. Which of these do you most often use? Which would you want others around you to use? Can you put them into any kind of order?

"The reality of the situation is…"
"I'll find a solution."
"I wasn't even aware that there was a problem."
"I'll wait and hope that someone else sorts it out."
"It's my problem too."
"It's her/his fault."
"I can't do it because…"
"I'll get on with it."

RESPONSIVE LEARNING

Once you have learned something and decided to change as a result of it, a number of reasonably predictable things begin to happen. Of course, they are much more complicated than the ones sketched out below. But there will, hopefully, be enough resonance with your own experiences for you to find this useful.

The goal for most organizations is to ensure that they have flexible, adaptable, optimistic employees. Most people recognize that flexibility and adaptability are key skills for their continued employment and personal success.

While it is easy to aspire to such goals, it is, of course, much more difficult to realize them! One way of preparing yourself is to be much clearer about the process of change and using the appropriate learning tools to thrive and adapt.

Use this chart to prompt your own thinking about the learning needed to support change effectively.

Stage	Other feelings, attitudes, and behaviors?	Kinds of learning needed to support the change
1 Early thinking, pioneering, and adventuring High excitement levels among senior people at the same time as anger, denial, resistance in some		
2 Refinement and improvement as the big picture is communicated more widely Excitement, engagement, fear, and resistance existing side by side		
3 Detailed plan agreed Confidence, excitement, nervousness, and more calculated resistance from a few		
4 Organization and individuals adapt as change is delivered Relief and gradual acceptance and ownership		
5 Consolidation of change at the same time as new business imperatives begin to appear Reflection, confidence, and determination linked to weariness		

RESPONSIVENESS—IN A NUTSHELL

YOU HAVE LEARNED:

✔ some principles of responsiveness
✔ how to manage change
✔ about the feelings that change produces in us
✔ how change is more effective when everybody is involved in the process and can respond accordingly

KEY IDEAS
Paradigm
WorkMats

14

Balancing Your Life

WE NEED TIME TO DEVELOP OUR MINDS. AND WE NEED TO HAVE OUR lives in balance if we are to be truly smart. As Honoré de Balzac wrote: "Time is the sole capital of people whose only fortune is their intelligence." As you have seen, learning is the most powerful aspect of human capital today.

Working hours are often long and, for many people, getting longer. Communication happens so quickly that people expect instant responses. It is as if the concept of the in-tray no longer exists. There is no place where data can sit until you are ready to deal with it. Telephones divert so easily from mobile to home to work and back again. Information seeps into our lives in an increasingly pervasive way.

We went through this when faxes were first invented. A letter sent by fax somehow seemed to be more important and urgent than a letter sent by the mail. Then there was voicemail. Now, when you record a message for someone, you somehow expect a reply more quickly than if you had left a message with a secretary. No sooner has an email arrived than there is a sense that it has to be answered. Many business people answer some of their emails at home or on the train to and from work. Copying emails indiscriminately is becoming a form of office terrorism. We can book holidays, order groceries, and check our investments over the internet at the touch of a button, wherever we are. All we have to remember the number of our credit card and its expiry date.

You already know how the wrong kind of stress adversely affects your mind. Indiscriminate email is undoubtedly causing the wrong kind of stress in too many people. For many people, the flow of data is like a surging current driving a powerful white water river, while we are on a small raft, hanging on for grim life hoping that we can stay afloat.

The boundaries between home and work are, for many people, also increasingly blurred. Flexible working patterns have created a new freedom for some workers. An increasing number of people work largely from home, especially in the fast-growing field of knowledge and communications companies. For these individuals, there may be a sense of more freedom and control over working time.

But, for many busy executives, emails at home and growing workloads are bad news for them, their partners, their friends, and their family. To keep your job, you work longer hours and send more emails to other people, who have to work longer to deal with them. You may be better off in terms of money, but you simply do not have enough time to develop.

It need not be like this.

In a survey in 2000 by British bank Lloyds TSB, men and women aged 16 and above were asked to cast an actor to play them in a film of their choice. Women overwhelmingly chose Judy Dench, who was perceived as being wise and charismatic. A close runner-up was Kate Winslet, who was more popular with younger women. The men were equally definite. Sean Connery was the outright winner, being seen as a man of integrity. He was followed by Al Pacino.

Those surveyed were also asked to say who exemplified a person who is living life to the full. Explorer Ranulph Fiennes topped the poll. In second and third places were UK media personality Chris Evans and international popstar Madonna. Only 9 percent of respondents thought that Bill Gates had a fulfilled life, while Richard Branson achieved a lowly 2 percent.

In addition, 61 percent of both sexes said that they would turn down a work promotion in order to enrich their personal life, whereas only 29 percent would accept one that might compromise their personal happiness. Work is, not surprisingly, even in today's materialistic world, a means to an end. Personal relationships are felt to be much more important than having money.

When asked what they would most like to be remembered for, people responded as follows:

Attribute	%
Sense of humor	82
Kindness	81
Generosity	75
Zest for life	65

Lloyds TSB group chief executive, Peter Ellwood, puts it like this:

Everyone has a life outside work, whether it is caring for children or elderly parents, studying or playing sport. Increasingly as employers we need to be able to help our employees to balance their work with the rest of their lives, if we are to be employers of choice.

In the UK there has been an interesting development in this area with the formation, in 1998, of the National Work-Life Forum. This has been set up in the belief that "helping men and women feel more in control of their lives is good for society and good for business." Working in partnership with government, employers, and a range of interested organizations to "make the case," the Forum is developing strategies that will help us successfully combine the demands of work with our personal, family, and community lives.

The campaign has attracted the support of Prime Minister Blair, who has said:

Millions of people across the UK would like to benefit from flexible ways of working. At the same time, the best businesses are showing that a better balance between work and life does not have to come at the expense of profits and competitiveness.

It is being trialed by a number of major companies, including Gemini Consulting, which is exploring the effect of introducing "quality of life" contracts and charters in some of its teams. Prudential Direct has set up home-based call centers linked to state-of-the-art automated data distribution systems, surely the way ahead for this kind of work.

There is the distinct feeling that, as John Bradshaw wrote, organizations are realizing: "You are a human being not a human doing; you are a human being not a human performance." This is good news for business and good news for all of us.

Stop and think for a moment about changes in your own life. What are the most important ones? In technology? In the pace of life? In your relationships? In society? In politics? In the world of work?

What does the organization you work for do to help people get the work–life balance right? What does it do that hinders them? What would you most like to change to improve things?

In 1999, the Campaign for Learning created Family Learning Weekend, a time when organizations all over the UK were encouraged to think more expansively of their personal and family learning needs. Hundreds of thousands of individuals took part in "taster" activities, and the event seems set to become a fixture in the calendar. Many businesses took the opportunity to think more broadly about their involvement in the wider community, including the families of their workforce.

A LIFE BALANCE QUIZ

Do you have your own life in balance? Try the following simple quiz to analyze the state of your own life at the moment.

The hours you keep

	A Never	B Sometimes	C Very often	D Always
1. Do you get home before 7pm?	❏	❏	❏	☑
2. Do you manage not to work on your journey to and from work?	❏	❏	❏	☑
3. Do you manage not to work at home in the evenings?	❏	☑	❏	❏
4. Do you manage not to work at weekends?	❏	☑	❏	❏

Your relationships

	A Never	B Sometimes	C Very often	D Always
5. Do you eat with your partner on weekday evenings?	❏	❏	☑	❏
6. Do you have time to talk to your partner before you go to work?	☑	❏	❏	❏
7. Do you take your child(ren) to school?	❏	❏	❏	❏
8. Do you pick up your child(ren) from school?	❏	❏	❏	❏
9. Do you help your child(ren) with their homework during the week?	❏	❏	❏	❏
10. Do you make love to your partner during the week?	❏	☑	❏	❏
11. Do you see friends during the week who are not also work colleagues?	❏	☑	❏	❏

Your interests

	A Never	B Sometimes	C Very often	D Always
12. Do you fit hobbies or interests into your life?	❏	☑	❏	❏
13. Do you make time to read for enjoyment rather than for work?	❏	❏	☑	❏
14. Do you listen to music?	❏	☑	❏	❏

Your health

	A Never	B Sometimes	C Very often	D Always
15. Do you take exercise?	❏	☑	❏	❏
16. Do you make time to reflect, think, or meditate during the week?	☑	❏	❏	❏
17. Do you choose to walk, rather than taking a car, bus, train, or taxi during the week?	☑	❏	❏	❏

	A¹ Never	B² Sometimes	C³ Very often	D⁴ Always
18. Do you manage to avoid being irritable with your partner/family when you get home from work?	☐	☐	☑	☐
19. Do you manage to avoid staying awake at night thinking about work?	☐	☐	☑	☐
20. Do you wake up feeling refreshed and well slept?	☐	☑	☐	☐

Score 1 for each box you have ticked under column A, 2 under B, 3 under C, and 4 under D. If you don't have a partner, answer those questions that apply. If you don't have children, miss out questions 7–9. If you work from home, adapt the questions as you think fit.

Analyzing your scores

64–80   Your life is very well balanced.

46–63   You are trying to concentrate on your home life as well as on your work.

28–45   There are times when your work is intruding into your life.

10–27   Your work is dominating your life.

All of the leaders I have interviewed are acutely conscious of the difficult balancing act involved in reconciling work and family lives. Most of them put some clear boundaries around weekends and some of their weekday time. But, most of them also work very long hours and travel extensively and internationally.

Several spoke of their partner as coach and critical friend. There is, clearly, no right or wrong way of doing relationships. But, at least the issue of how people spend their time is beginning to be discussed more openly and sympathetically.

Brian Dyson, chief executive of Coca-Cola Enterprises, describes the challenge of today's hectic life:

Imagine life as a game in which you are juggling some five balls in the air. You name them—work, family, health, friends and spirit—and you're

keeping all of these in the air. You will soon understand that work is a rub-
ber ball. If you drop it, it will bounce back. But the other four balls—fam-
ily, health, friends and spirit—are made of glass. If you drop one of these,
they will become irrevocably scuffed, marked, nicked, damaged, or even
shattered. They will never be the same. You must understand that and
strive for balance in your life.

CONTROLLING STRESS

Of course, all human beings are prone to failure under pressure.
Racing drivers make inexplicable decisions, sports people of all
kinds suddenly lose a match they have seemed to be winning, chief
executives suddenly start making odd decisions, and talented people of all kinds fail when they are doing things at which they have
always excelled in the past.

Malcolm Gladwell has explored two particularly useful concepts here, the ideas of choking and panicking. You have already
seen how, under conditions of extreme stress, the higher-order functions of the brain simply stop functioning properly. A rhino is charg-
ing at you and all thoughts of philosophy or business economics, not
surprisingly, desert you as you seek to survive.

Nevertheless, in everyday life it may be helpful to divide
these experiences into two different categories, the moment when
you "choke" and the moment when you panic. Choking is possibly
the more common of the two experiences.

Gladwell's example of choking is of Jana Novotna's 1993
Wimbledon tennis final against Steffi Graf. At one moment on the
point of winning the match, Novotna suddenly and inexplicably
lost her touch and let Graf overtake her and win the tournament.
Novotna, in short, choked. Perhaps because of the enormity of the
event or the presence of the crowd, she simply started to think too
much about what she was doing. Consequently, her play became
labored and too self-conscious. She lost the easy familiarity of her
strokes and became increasingly agitated.

On page 79 you explored the idea of conscious and unconscious competence. The example given was of an experienced car

driver who no longer even thinks about their actions as they move the steering wheel and manipulate the pedals. Such a person is no longer conscious of their competence or skill, they do it, as it were, on automatic pilot. It seems that your basal ganglia in your mammalian or middle brain is probably partly responsible for the development of this kind of unconscious or tacit learning.

It is the same with tennis or any activity demanding high levels of performance. If you are too stressed, it is possible that you will stop functioning at an unconscious level and revert to the much more mechanical, conscious one that you displayed as you were learning the skill. In this type of situation, you are simply thinking too much. If you are able to do so, the cure for your stress is to think less, to seek to recapture the instinctive version of your performance.

A good example that I have experienced is public speaking. I do a lot of this and am generally told that I am pretty good at it. But just occasionally, for no obviously scientific reason, I have a choking experience. Somebody in the audience says something that niggles me, or perhaps I am already feeling stressed from a bad journey, and I choke. Suddenly, I try too hard, my stories become labored, and my delivery becomes stilted. I have gone back a stage in the learning process and am now operating as if my competence in public speaking had only just been acquired and was very much at the conscious level. I know now that the way out of this is not to try even harder; quite the reverse. I need to create a short space for myself, by having a drink of water or asking the audience to do something, so that I can catch my breath. In this way, I find that I can recapture the more natural, unconscious level of operation.

Panicking is different. To continue with the example of public speaking, if you panic in situations like this, although it may still be a kind of failure as far as your audience is concerned, what is going on inside your head is quite different. I can remember the feelings of panic when I was just starting to learn the craft of speaking a decade ago. In this situation, your mind goes blank. You cannot remember what it was that you were going to say. The stressful nature of the situation is effectively removing your short-term memory. The problem is that you have stopped thinking and are experiencing what psychologists refer to as "perceptual narrowing." You stop noticing the full range of experience around you.

The thing to do in this kind of case is to give yourself props to rely on if you feel an onset of panic. These could include a visual map of your talk, the first few words written out in full, some good quotations to use if the going gets tough, and many other things to help you through the situation and give you recovery time to start thinking again.

Another classic example of panic would be of a diver in trouble under the sea. On breathing in, they discover that they are inhaling water and not air. They stop thinking and grab at the nearest air supply, even if it is attached to someone else, in the fevered attempt to find oxygen. They panic. Even though in all their training they have been taught to try to share another's air supply and gradually return to the surface, all memory of this deserts them.

Both choking and panicking lead to a reduction in performance. However, while their effect may appear to be the same to someone watching, what is going on in your head is quite different. Most importantly, the cures are different. When you choke you need to think less; when you panic you need to think more.

Think of times when you have choked or panicked. What caused you to do this?
What did you do to deal with the situation?
What tends to make you choke or panic in your work or home lives today? Think of some positive strategies for dealing with these situations.

Of course, there is such a thing as useful stress. This is the stress that ensures that we get out of bed each morning and that the targets we set ourselves have an impact on our daily lives. We are all different, however. What for one person would be an acceptable level of stress, for another would be health threatening. Much of our reaction to stress depends on our attitude to events. You saw in the last chapter how change inevitably brings stress and how anticipating some of the feelings associated with it can minimize the negative aspects. You also learned on page 46 about the critical concepts of learned optimism and pessimism.

The key concept in managing stress is the idea of taking control. Jayne-Anne Gadhia was the most forthright of those I interviewed about this subject: "I am stressed if I am not in control or if I am not well organized."

Indeed, for many people, helplessness is a major contributor to stress. What is important is to work out what you can do something about and what you are not able to influence. The most stressful moments are those over which we feel we have no control. When we are stranded on a railway station late at night and the last train is canceled, for example, we feel helpless rage. When we are desperately trying to produce papers for an important meeting or against an external deadline and the photocopier jams, we may experience a rage of impotent desperation. But, even in these situations we can minimize the stress. A call home to reassure your family, or a decision to pay out on an expensive taxi or to call a friend and ask to stay the night, if taken quickly, stops us sinking into frightened inactivity. Or, early decisions to redeploy other staff, use another copier, or go to an outside copy shop can reduce the angst associated with the inevitability of mechanical failure. At a deeper level, the application of double-loop thinking (see page 174) can provide more creative system options to many of the predictable life experiences.

When we are under great stress, we want to fight or run away. Stress is at the heart of ensuring our successful survival as a species. We have to decide whether to stay or go off to pastures new. Biologically, our heart starts beating up to five times faster and our adrenal gland produces cortisol. Our blood vessels expand to ensure better blood circulation, our pupils dilate for better sight, and our digestive system is shut down through the narrowing of the blood vessels that feed the organs involved in digestion. All of this is controlled by the hypothalamus in our brain. If the incident of stress is short lived, our biological systems return to normal and no harm is done. If it is prolonged, we suffer from all the well-known stress-related illnesses: ulcers, bowel diseases, depression, loss of memory, and a reduced immune system.

Luckily, there are many symptoms you can spot before you start to suffer more seriously. Here are just a few:

- Irritability
- Aggressiveness
- Overdefensiveness
- Indecisiveness
- Poor concentration
- Lack of self-confidence
- Prolonged tiredness
- Tension in muscles, especially the neck, shoulders, and back
- Headaches
- Indigestion
- Insomnia
- Constipation
- Sweating profusely

This is a frightening list. But, don't worry: it might not be stress that is causing them, but something like going to bed too late, alcohol, or the many other things we are all attracted by!

So, in a stressful situation, we either run or fight, literally or metaphorically. Sometimes we are caught in between, frozen into helplessness, without the ability to think constructively about the best course of action. As American business thinker Michael Hammer puts it: "It's exhilarating to be stretched to your limit, but after a while you need a break before you break."

What are the most stressful things going on for you at the moment?

Do you recognize any of these symptoms in your life? Start to think about what is causing these symptoms.

Think about what is going on for you at work, about your workload, about those who work closely with you, about your sense of being valued, about your ability to manage your time.

Think about new developments that are worrying you.

Think about how you communicate with others and they with you.

Think about the resources at your disposal.

What about your life outside work, in the community, at home?

Is your overall financial situation causing you to worry?

The first of four important steps in dealing with stress is to be much clearer about what you are stressed about. Once you have generated a list of these try the following:

1   Draw a line down the middle of a piece of paper, creating two halves. Label the left-hand side "Worries" and the right-hand side "What I could do." Write all your worries on the left and think of all the things you could do to help overcome them. At this stage, do not get diverted into thinking about how you might improve matters. This is a recipe for confused thinking and subsequent inaction. Focus instead on what you could do. List even those things you think you have tried already.

2   Pick out the three most important worries you have and label them 1, 2, or 3 in another color.

    You now have the beginnings of some more detailed self-analysis, rather than the generalized sense of stress that can be so damaging to us all. The next stage is to select one of your top three worries and generate some positive actions for it:

3   Focus on each of your main three worries in turn. Still concentrating on what you might do not how you might do it, for each one agree with yourself one thing that you are going to do. Say it to yourself in the privacy of your head. Then, sleep on your ideas and say them to yourself again on the next day. As you gain in confidence with these tentative ideas, start to tell other people what you are going to do.

4   Now, start to think about how you are going to implement some of the things you have thought of. Use some of the creative thinking techniques in Chapter 9 to help you.

    As well as focusing on your own needs, there are some simple things you can do in the workplace to minimize the negative effects of stress on you, your mind, and the minds of your colleagues. How much you can do personally may depend to some extent on your seniority.

Nevertheless, there are often things we can all do simply by articulating a suggestion that will clearly be something that benefits everyone. These kinds of ideas are actually quite difficult to ignore, even in the least creative workplaces!

10 ways of cutting down stress at work

1   Create conditions where employees have maximum control over their working lives, for example, by sharing as much information as possible or by encouraging teams to manage themselves.

2   Offer learning opportunities for all staff, including some time that can be used for personal development.

3   Ensure that every employee thinks about their goals for the week ahead a week before, and their goals for tomorrow the day before or early on the day in question.

4   Establish a culture where it is expected that individuals will ask for help throughout the day if they are unable to prioritize their own workload.

5   Create flexible work arrangements for as many staff as possible.

6   Encourage employees to take physical exercise, learn yoga, auto-genic training, meditation, sitting posture, regular breathing, and other useful techniques, by laying on sessions before and after the working day or in the lunch break.

7   Encourage people to take breaks by taking them yourself.

8   Encourage everyone to share their one favorite stress buster and display these as posters or on your intranet.

9   Tell jokes, encourage laughter, and actively seek to find the funny side in all that goes on at work.

10   Spend the last hour of the day on the least stressful things, for example, making some nice telephone calls, thinking about the next day, or tidying up. Give yourself a few minutes of quiet reflection before you return through your front door at home, by stopping the car a few miles away, listening to music in the car, train, or bus, stopping to look at a view if you are walking, and actively "switching off" your work mind before you "rejoin" your personal world. Avoid leaving that one last call so that it has to be done in your first few minutes back home!

A DIFFERENT KIND OF LIFE PLANNING

It has been an argument throughout this book that everything connects. Mind and body. Body and spirit. Feelings and thoughts. Science and living. Learning and change. Work and home lives. To be fulfilled and successful in today's complex world involves learning to learn and using your mind to its full potential.

At the heart of achieving this is the need to take control of your own life. Feeling helpless is a stressful and unhealthy state of being. Organizations recognize this, which is why they produce business plans. These seek to reflect the priorities of those working within them. They try to make sure that time is spent on what matters for the organization. But, what about you as an individual in your private life? How much time do you spend setting your own priorities and ensuring that they are understood and shared by those to whom you are close?

Stephen Covey explored the idea of creating a Family Mission Statement in *The 7 Habits of Highly Effective Families.* "Being proactive" is the first of the seven habits he seeks to encourage. There are many interesting and detailed suggestions for putting your mission into practice as a family. However, I suspect that many busy business people see a book like that and think that it is about self-improvement and not, therefore, relevant to their working lives. I want to suggest a simple approach to getting your personal life priorities in order, which is, paradoxically for some business people, central to being successful in life.

Its premise is simplicity itself. Unless you are happy and doing the things that are important to you in your private life, you cannot be truly successful in your working life.

Since our marriage in 1995, for both of us a second marriage, my wife and I have been spending a great deal of time seeking to understanding our priorities and living these out together. We have evolved a set of approaches that are personal to us, but I hope that even if you throw up your hands in horror at some of the ideas, you might find enough resonance in what I am saying to want to develop something that works for you and your partner, or simply for yourself if you are on your own at the moment.

Once a year—over a couple of weekends in the summer—we invest time in looking back over the year, taking stock of where we are, and planning forward for the coming months. As a result of this, we produce a Family Life Plan. It has taken different forms for the last five years, but it is essentially a map and set of instructions for the next phase of our lives together. It is like a business plan in that it describes what we want to do, but it is quite unlike any business plan I have ever seen when it comes to its mode of expression and the emphasis it places on values and feelings.

The process goes something like this. It has seven stages. I have assumed that you will be sharing this with your partner, but it might be possible for an individual to use these ideas to prompt discussions about their life with a close friend:

1. Set one whole weekend aside when you will not be disturbed by family or friends

2. Plan to do some of the things you most enjoy doing together and, while you are doing these things, make lots of time to talk, listen, learn, feel, and think

3. Start by looking back over the highs and lows of the last year and taking stock

4. Talk about and agree where you currently think you want to get to in your lives and what you need in order to do this that you do not currently have

5. Focus on what you want to do in the next twelve months

6. Focus on how you can do what you want to do in the next twelve months

7. Produce some kind of written or pictorial record of how and when you are going to do what you have agreed that you want to do

Stage 1: Making space

It is really important that you invest time in this activity. If one of you does not want to do it and is there under sufferance, it will not work. Similarly, if either of your minds is elsewhere on other things, you will not find it a fulfilling experience. So, the first time you do it, you really need to be sure that you are both committed to spending a good stretch of time just exploring yourselves. We find that the first weekend back in the real world after the summer holidays works well for us. We are relaxed and the world of work is a reality again, but not an intrusive one. Grandparents or friends can often be persuaded to look after children to ensure that you can have private time.

Stage 2: The medium is the message

Doing what you like doing while you are talking about doing what you would like to do is a satisfying experience. In our case, we particularly enjoy walking, eating, and drinking together, so these activities feature strongly on our list. One year we chose to see a film that we thought might provoke some interesting lines of thought. Traveling away for a weekend might stimulate you to make connections. Or, you may prefer the familiarity of your own home.

Stage 3: Getting started

You might like to use the questionnaire about your work–life balance as a starting point for discussion. Or, you could look at some photographs or video footage of the previous year. Perhaps there are some particular items carrying special meaning for you that you would enjoy reviewing. We find it is essential at this stage to give each other private quiet space so that the initial thoughts and feelings we may be about to share are absolutely our own and not influenced by the other person. The simple idea of dividing a sheet of paper into two columns works well for us:

Things I have felt good about this year	Things I have not enjoyed this year

We then share these. All relationships have their disagreements and your list will inevitably be different from your partner's. So, it is very important to avoid any sense of blame here. You are simply stating what it felt like to you. Sometimes it may hurt when you hear what your partner says to you, because you will know you were partly to blame for what happened. In that case, try this response: "Thanks for telling me that. I did not realize you felt so strongly. What could I have done that would have helped you to...?"

Out of your highs and lows you need to produce a shared list, or two lists if you cannot agree. Now, stand back and look at what you have enjoyed most. What were the common factors? Do the same for the negative things. We find that regrouping our joint list into:

Things we would like to do more of   **Things we would like to do less of**

at this stage sets us up well for the next stage. Give yourself a break! You might like to classify the activities you have been talking about, using descriptive language that helps you better articulate your feelings.

When you are rested, you may like to take stock of two kinds of accounts, your Family Balance Sheet and your Emotional Bank Account.

The Family Balance Sheet is the easier of the two to work out. If you can persuade yourself to take time to grapple with this issue, you will have a firm financial base from which you can view your situation.

Most couples have a clear sense of what comes into their bank every month or year and what goes out. Often, it is a struggle to reconcile the two figures! But, what about the underlying picture? It is helpful to try to work this out. When you have done it once it will be much easier to have a realistic sense of how much you are worth.

Do you own part or all of your house? If so, how much equity do you hold? Do you own shares? If so, how much are they worth? Do you have investments, for example, endowment policies and other financial products that will yield you an income in the future? Do you own any other large items, like cars, caravans, pictures, or antiques? Do you have a pension? When will it be available to you? How much will it be worth? It is worth valuing these and then adjusting their value in subsequent years.

Your Balance Sheet may look something like this:

Family Balance Sheet	£ or $
House	
Car	
Savings	
Investments, including pension	
Other items	
Total	

Since reading Stephen Covey's book, we have started to include the wonderful concept of the Family Emotional Bank Account. As Covey writes, "The Emotional Bank Account represents the quality of the relationship you have with others." In this case, you would be interested in the quality of your own relationship. Now that you have started to think about money, you will find it easier to make the connections between an account and the important issue of your emotions. Every time you do something positive for your partner—express your love, help them out, do something extra for them—you are making a deposit in their Emotional Bank Account. Each time you hurt your partner or disregard their feelings, you make a withdrawal from their Emotional Bank Account.

In a normal joint account you receive one statement of the total balance. Think of this as a different kind of account, one in which each person receives a different statement. If you have been giving a lot to your loved one, their statement will show you to be well in credit. If you have been thoughtless, grumpy, and selfish, your statement will show that you have a low fund balance.

The idea, of course, is for you both to feel that you have made significant deposits. That way, when times get tough, you can make withdrawals, consciously depending on the emotional support of your partner.

You don't want to find that the account is empty when you need to do this—what you do after sharing the idea of the account is more important than working out who is in credit or not! It can be a really helpful way of beginning to understand your partner's feelings about a range of matters. You will need to give more than you take at this stage.

Stage 4: Agreeing a common destination

Have you ever stopped to work out where you both want to go? Do you want to be in the same job in ten years' time? What do you want to have achieved in your life? Do you want to work for ever? If one of you is currently looking after the family, what are your plans?

Flicking through magazines and selecting pictures that mean something to you can be a good way of stimulating discussion. Talking about people you admire and why you admire them can help. Creating an "If only" list may give you some ideas. Telling stories to each other might be fun, imagining a fantasy world in which your wildest dreams can be realized. Sharing dreams is helpful.

Playing "If I were you I might..." works well if things are going well. Agreeing to differ and "to give that some serious thought" works well if you seem to be moving apart.

Take stock of what your destinations have in common. What do you need to get to your dreams? What can you do to support your partner in realizing their goals?

Stage 5: Reality intrudes, but not completely

So, what are you going to do together in the coming year? On no account drift into how you are going to do it yet.

Start with the big things, the principles. These for us have been things like:

◆   Spending more time together during weekday evenings.
◆   Spending time with our most special friends.
◆   Working shorter hours.
◆   Finding out what it would be like to work for ourselves.
◆   Eating more organic food.

Then, think about the different areas of your life. See if you can agree one or two things you are going to do under each heading. Headings might be drawn from these kind of words: Us together,

Family, Friends, Home, Garden, Holidays, Money, Health, Leisure, Spiritual, and, of course, Learning and Development.

Stage 6: Reality intrudes

If things have gone well, this is the most enjoyable part of the process as you realize just how much of your life you can take control of. Merely hearing yourself saying that you are going to stop doing some things and start doing others is intoxicating stuff! We found it helpful to rehearse some of the situations from which we are trying to extricate ourselves using role play. It can be lots of fun.

One of the main skills you may need to develop as a couple is the art of saying no without giving offense, especially when you are tying to break certain patterns of behavior.

Stage 7: Committing to the plan

It is psychologically very important that you both actively engage in making an agreed record of what you are planning to do.

Let your imagination run riot or do it very simply, whichever you prefer. But do commit yourself in words and, possibly, in pictures to what you are going to do next year.

It is helpful to enjoy revisiting your plan several times during the year to see how things are going for you.

BALANCING YOUR LIFE—IN A NUTSHELL

YOU HAVE LEARNED:

✔ how work–home boundaries are blurring
✔ about the importance of life outside work
✔ about the state of your own work–life balance
✔ how to manage stress effectively

KEY IDEAS
Family Balance Sheet
Emotional Bank Account

KEY TECHNIQUES/ APPROACHES
Life balance quiz
Stress management
Life planning

15
Making Time for Learning

Whenit comes down to it, learning is no different from anything else you might do in your busy life. It competes for your attention with things like work, family, eating, shopping, television, and sex. How you manage your time is therefore of the utmost importance. Learning is the activity that does most to develop your brain, the most important organ in your body. You therefore need to make time for it. Of course, you have to exercise and feed your body, but you also have to do the same with your brain. As Bob Fryer, the prime architect of the UK's lifelong learning strategy, puts it, you have to "make learning normal."

MAKING LEARNING NORMAL

This is not a book about time management, but it may be helpful to spend a few minutes thinking about how you can make sure you use your time in the way you want. Books and courses about time management rightly stress the need to focus on the things that are important to you, not the ones that happen to come up as opportunities.

To work this out with regard to your own learning, there are two stages. The first involves analyzing the activities of your current life and those you are planning or considering, and the second requires you to set goals and break them down into achievable elements. Once you have done this, you can begin to plan.

What does a typical week in your life look like? How much of it is spent trying to learn things? Obviously, you learn without being conscious of it, so it may be difficult to be sure.

Use the week at a view chart below to work out how much time you spend doing things. The kinds of things you might want to include on your weekly chart are work, domestic chores, sports, gardening, DIY, playing with family, time with your partner, eating, television, courses you take, traveling to and from work, etc.

Once you have got a clear idea of how you spend your week, group the activities under five or six headings, one of which is learning, and make a personal pie chart to show how much time you spend on each of them.

	Monday	Tuesday	Wednesday	Thursday	Friday	Saturday	Sunday
Work	8 hours						
Chores	1 hour						
Sports	1 hour						
Family	2 hours						
Travel	1 hour						
Learning	1 hour etc.						

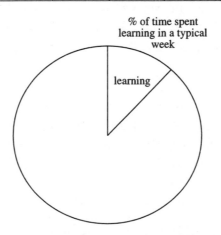

% of time spent learning in a typical week

learning

In time management courses, a typical activity at this stage would be to classify these activities into those that are urgent and those that are important. Most of us spend far too much time doing things that seem urgent but are not in fact very important.

I don't think that this is a rigorous enough way of dealing with your learning. There are other factors that need to be taken into account.

WHY YOU NEED A LEARNING PRACTITIONER

In most societies, the notion of the apprentice used to be strongly embedded. It is, in a sense, a potent reminder of the normality of learning. If you wanted to be a printer, you did not go on a training course, you became apprenticed to a printer. If you wished to learn to dye clothes, you spent a number of years with a dyer, and so on. The same is true in our personal lives. We watch, imitate, and learn from our parents. We are apprentice cooks, cleaners, carers, and partners, with them as our home tutors.

Interestingly, having abandoned the concept a decade or so ago, Britain has successfully reintroduced the idea of apprenticeship as a means of learning, by creating a Modern Apprenticeship scheme.

Who we learn with is one of the most powerful influences on our learning. The truth is, we all need help: we all need learning friends just as we need friends in our social life.

When we were concerned about improving the health of the British nation early in the twentieth century, we invented a network of doctors called GPs (general practitioners). Everyone had the right to be registered with a GP, free of charge. I believe the time has come for each person to have an LP or learning practitioner as a "critical friend" throughout their life. LPs could be to the mind what GPs are to our bodies.

This could be an experienced coach or a mentor. It could be a godparent or grandparent. It could be a professional friend in another organization. It could be your partner. It could be a teacher, tutor, or librarian. It could be a midwife or social worker. It could be a therapist of some kind. It could be a work colleague.

Many of you will, as well as having a doctor, have access to an independent financial adviser. In the Knowledge Age, you need access to a learning practitioner. Of course, the LP concept is a much looser one than these examples from health or financial services might suggest.

The essential characteristics of the LP include the following:

- They need to be focused on your needs unconditionally for the period that they are working with you.
- They need to have some basic understanding of how you can learn to learn more effectively.
- They need to be a critical friend to you, supporting you, challenging you, and giving you specific and constructive feedback.
- They need to be able to listen to you and draw out your plans, helping you to own these and set them in motion, as appropriate.

Given the brain's capacity for imitation, your choice of LP is obviously an extremely important one, as is your choice of who you spend most of your time with at work and in your private life. They will undoubtedly be a huge influence on you, your mind, and the way you think, feel, and believe.

It is my personal crusade for the first decade of the twenty-first century to persuade at least one national government that this is a good idea. In my view, such a scheme would transform the effectiveness of people and help them to realize more of their hidden talents. It would be comparatively inexpensive, as much of it would be undertaken on a voluntary basis or as part of an existing job.

Have you had an LP of any kind? What is she or he like? How do they help you? What other characteristics would you suggest they should have?

The British Industrial Society went further in a report published in 2000 aimed at improving the quality of working life: "Employers should give their staff more room to enjoy their work. Instead of seeing sociability at work as the antithesis of efficiency and productivity they should see it as crucial to the bottom line. Gossip is the cement which holds organizations together."

You will know that, in terms of the science of the brain, this is only partially true. While we certainly benefit from social interaction and the informal learning that flows from it, malicious gossip can be harmful. Our brain's tendency to complete the picture means that we draw our own conclusions, often unnecessarily and stressfully thinking the worst! So, combine an organization that really keeps its employees informed about what is happening and what is being considered with one that encourages lots of informal chat and you have a winning formula. Many organizations are beginning to realize this and providing attractive physical spaces where workers want to eat and drink.

> How much do you encourage or take part in informal learning in your workplace? Or, if you work from home, what networks are you part of?
>
> If you are in a position of responsibility, try giving your team money to have drinks or food together once a month. They will almost inevitably share work issues and come up with useful solutions that will justify such apparently irresponsible generosity.

MAKING A PERSONAL LEARNING ACTION PLAN

In the 1990s, Sir Christopher Ball, then chairman of the British Campaign for Learning, suggested that everyone should have a plan for their learning. The version on the next few pages is inspired by the early model that he created.

Taking stock

1. My most enjoyable learning in my life so far has been:

Example   When   Where   How   Why

2. The things I am best at are:

Examples   The intelligence(s) I am using for this are:

3. My preferred learning style is:

Eyes, Ears or Body?   Activist, Reflector, Theorist, Pragmatist?

4. The three intelligences I would most like to develop further are:

Intelligence   Reason

5. The place I most like to learn in is:

6. The times I like to learn best are:

Time   Reason

7. The ways I prefer to learn are:

Method   Reason
1
2
3

My wish list

8. The things I want to achieve in the next three years are:

Home	Work	Social	Personal	Other

9. The things that are changing most in my life are:

1
2
3

To survive and thrive during these changes, I need to learn:

1
2
3

10. The gap between where I want to be and what I can do now is:

Competence ├─┼─┼─┼─┼─┼─┼─┼─┼─┼─┤ Goal

11. The things I need to learn are:

Home	Work
Social	Personal
Other	

12. The things I plan to learn are:

What	Why	How	When	Where
1				
2				
3				

This is how I will know if I have been successful:

MAKING TIME FOR LEARNING—IN A NUTSHELL

YOU HAVE LEARNED:

✔ that to make learning a regular and normal part of your life requires careful planning
✔ how to make a personal learning action plan

KEY IDEAS
Learning practitioner
Personal learning action plan

KEY TECHNIQUE/ APPROACH
Using a personal learning action plan

Part IV

Useful Information

An A–Z of Brain-Based Approaches to Life and Work

A   Asking for help is essential or you will get stuck. Your brain likes to be Adventurous. It is also constantly Adapting.

B   You need to get the Big picture or you will not be able to connect to what you are learning. Brainstorming is good for suspending judgment early in the creative process and tends to produce more original ideas toward the end of the session.

C   Chunking your learning helps you to deal with it in manageable bits, and builds in lots of beginnings and endings so you will remember more. Curiosity is essential, as is Challenge, on which your brain thrives.

D   Dialog is one of the most effective ways of communicating and engaging with people.

E   Unless you are Emotionally ready to learn, the learning will not stick. Exercise is important, both physical and mental. The Environment dramatically affects how you learn. You learn through Experience.

F   Feedback is very important. Without it your mind cannot be sure how it is doing! Failure is an important and necessary element of learning. It is a kind of feedback.

G   Generosity is an important attribute. In a generous culture, self-respect grows, creativity is encouraged, and experimentation is seen as part of the process of learning.

H   Hydration is essential to the effective operation of the brain. Humor helps people to relax and improves your ability to think and remember.

I   Your brain is programmed to Imitate others. Creative Imitation is an essential part of learning. The caliber of your role models is very important.

J   Joy is essential in life. Without it there is no purpose to living or learning.

K   The Kinesthetic or physical approach to learning and the taking in of information is much underused in the workplace. Getting up off your seat also has the effect of energizing your brain.

L   Listening is an important skill for learners. Learning practitioners can help you to learn more effectively, and knowing about your preferred Learning style will help you know what you can do to become a more developed learner.

M   Music aids relaxation and can improve memory. Mistakes are an inevitable and helpful element of learning. Your own Motivation is a critical element of your success as a learner.

N   Your "Natural intelligence" is your capacity to learn how to learn. As such, it is your most important asset!

O   Optimism is an essential attribute and can be learned.

P   Practical intelligence is an under-rated commodity. Praise helps you to remain motivated. Your brain loves Patterns.

Q   Questioning is an important skill. You need some Quiet in your learning life.

R   The 5Rs are Resourcefulness, Remembering, Resilience, Reflectiveness, and Responsiveness.

S   Sleep and Stretch breaks keep your brain healthy. Exploring your Spiritual intelligence may help you to gain control of your life. Self-esteem is essential in the learning process.

T   As well as a full Toolkit of techniques, you need Time to reflect and process your learning.

U   Sometimes you have to Unlearn what you learned in school and elsewhere.

V   About a third of us prefer to take in information Visually, a third, with our ears, and a third through direct experience.

W   The Web is a source of great learning and great confusion.

X   There must be a good use for X-rays, but I haven't thought of it yet!

Y   Learning to learn is about You and your success in life.

Z   Z is for Zaniness, essential in today's business world.

TROUBLESHOOTING

Here are some solutions to some common problems you may encounter while using your mind. Provided that you follow the suggestions in Part I, you are unlikely to experience serious difficulties. The most common source of trouble is careless treatment of the brain or the body in which it is packed!

You don't know what kind of learner you are

Possible cause	What to do
Nobody has ever told you that each person has natural preferences about the way they learn.	Work out whether you are an activist, reflector, theorist, or pragmatist by looking at page 97, and then decide whether you prefer to take in information with your ears, your eyes, or by trying it out.

You can't seem to absorb information

Possible causes	What to do
You are tired.	Try to get at least seven and a half hours' sleep.
You are being talked at.	Seek a more interactive approach to your learning.
You have not really connected.	Make sure you ask for and get the big picture.

You can't get started

Possible causes	What to do
You don't really want to get started.	Think more carefully about why you want to undertake the learning, the new opportunities it will give you.

Possible causes	What to do
You have temporarily lost your sense of curiosity.	Stop watching so much television! Plan to spend an evening doing something you have never done before.
You are under too much stress.	Your mind is elsewhere, worrying about something else. Work out what the something else is and what you could do about it to improve things. Ask for help from someone you trust.
Your environment is wrong.	Prepare a special place to learn at home or at work where you feel really good and where you have all the equipment you need at your fingertips. Turn off all mobile phones and put other phones on voicemail.

Your mind does not seem motivated to learn

Possible causes	What to do
You had awful experiences of learning at school.	So did many other people! But learning need not be like it was at school. Use what you know about learning styles to select something that really suits you.
You are not really certain that you want to do the learning.	Use the formula on page 63, $R + V + P + I = M$, to work out your motivation. If it is not high enough, think again!
You are going for the wrong topic!	Use the plan on page 246 to help you be sure that your learning is going to help you do what you want to do.
You are being too hard on yourself.	Take a break. Celebrate what you have done so far. Ask a friend for their advice.

Possible causes	What to do
You are trying to be too ambitious.	Break what you are trying to learn up into manageable chunks.

There is no time to learn

Possible cause	What to do
You have not stopped to work out how important your planned learning is to you.	Complete a personal learning action plan.

You keep getting stuck

Possible cause	What to do
You do not have enough strategies for coping when the going gets tough.	Read Chapter 6 for some good ideas.

Your memory does not work properly

Possible causes	What to do
You are trying to remember too much.	Break it up into smaller chunks. You are more likely to remember the beginnings and endings of what you learn!
You have not made the connections.	Try to find the patterns or connections between the things you have learned by classifying them in ways that work for you.
You need to take a different kind of notes.	Try mind maps or free notes, see page 123.
You are tired.	Sleep on it.
Your learning is too passive.	Make it more active!

Possible causes	What to do
You are not fixing it in your brain carefully enough.	Review things regularly, after an hour, a day, and a month. Try muttering, see page 129.

You can't be creative at work

Possible causes	What to do
Too many of the seven seriously uncreative sins are on display.	Leave. Or find some like-minded people who can work with you to change the organization from within.
Your full range of intelligences is not being realized.	Read Chapter 9 for ideas on how you might do this.

You don't know how to be creative

Possible cause	What to do
Nobody has ever taught you how to think creatively.	Try some of the ideas in Chapter 9.

You are terrified of change

Possible cause	What to do
You are human! If we are truthful, most of us find change challenging. But you don't need to be terrified.	Try some of the approaches on page 218.

You don't know how to change

Possible cause	What to do
You have always been a passive recipient of change.	Take control! Learn to predict some of the feelings that commonly go along with change. Use some of the ideas on page 211.

You constantly have low energy

Possible causes	What to do
You are stressed.	Put yourself through the simple quiz on page 223 and do something about it! Listen to music.
You are doing things you don't really want to do.	Try the family planning activity on page 234. Review your spiritual self.
Your diet is poor.	Try to eat a more balanced diet, as suggested on page 22–4. Drink more water and less alcohol and coffee.
You are not taking enough exercise.	Remedy this!

You are working for too many hours

Possible cause	What to do
Your life is out of balance.	Be realistic about the tough situation you are in at the moment. But, within a definite timescale, no more than a month from now, adopt some of the suggestions in Part III.

RESOURCES

You may find the following books helpful:

Gillian Butler and Tony Hope, *Manage Your Mind: The Mental Fitness Guide*, Oxford Paperbacks, 1995.

Tony Buzan, *Use Your Head*, BBC Consumer Publishing, 2000.

Guy Claxton, *Wise Up: The Challenge of Lifelong Learning*, Bloomsbury, 2000.

Guy Claxton, *Hare Brain, Tortoise Mind: Why Intelligence Increases When You Think Less*, Fourth Estate, 2000.

Stephen Covey, *The Seven Habits of Highly Effective Families*, Simon & Schuster, 1999.

Mihaly Csikszentmihalyi, *Creativity: Flow and the Psychology of Discovery and Invention*, Harper Perennial, 1997.

Gordon Dryden and Jeanette Vos, *The Learning Revolution*, Jalmar Press, 1999.

Howard Gardner, *Frames of Mind: The Theory of Multiple Intelligences*, Basic Books, 1993.

Arie de Geus, *The Living Company: Growth, Learning and Longevity in Business*, Nicholas Brealey Publishing, 1999.

Daniel Goleman, *Emotional Intelligence: Why it Can Matter More than IQ*, Bloomsbury, 1996.

Susan Greenfield, *Brain Story*, BBC Consumer Publishing, 2000.

Susan Greenfield, *The Private Life of the Brain*, Penguin Books, 2001.

Carla Hannaford, *Smart Moves: Why Learning Is Not All in Your Head*, Great Ocean Publishers, 1995.

Peter Honey and Alan Mumford, *The Learning Styles Questionnaire: 80 item version*, Peter Honey Learning, 2000.

Pierce Howard, *The Owner's Manual for the Brain: Everyday Applications from Mind-Brain Research*, Bard Press, 2000.

Eric Jensen, *The Learning Brain*, Brain Store, 1994.

Otto Kroeger and Janet Thuesen, *Type Talk: The 16 Personality Types that Determine How We Live, Love and Work*, Dell Publishing, 1989.

Bill Lucas and Toby Greany, *Learning to Learn: Setting the Agenda for Schools in the 21st Century*, Campaign for Learning, 2000.

Bill Lucas and Toby Greany, *Schools in the Learning Age*, Campaign for Learning/Southgate Publishers, 2000.

Steven Mithen, *The Prehistory of the Mind: A Search for the Origins of Art, Religion and Science*, Phoenix Press, 1998.

Jonas Ridderstråle and Kjell Nordstrom, *Funky Business, Talent Makes Capital Dance*, Financial Times Prentice Hall, 2000.

Colin Rose and Malcom Nicholl, *Accelerated Learning for the 21st Century*, Dell Publishing, 1997.

Martin Seligman, *Learned Optimism: How to Change Your Mind and Your Life*, Pocket Books, 1998.

Danah Zohar and Ian Marshall, *SQ: The Ultimate Intelligence*, Bloomsbury, 1999.

Here are a few useful organizations:

Accelerated Learning Systems Ltd, 50 Aylesbury Road, Aston Clinton, Aylesbury, Bucks, HP22 5AH, UK
www.accelerated-learning-uk.co.uk

Campaign for Learning, 19 Buckingham Street, London, WC2N 6EF, UK
www.campaign-for-learning.org.uk and www.learntolearn.org

Celemi UK, Compass House, Priestley Road, Surrey Research Park, Guildford, Surrey, UK
www.celemi.com

Herrmann International, PO Box 1, Battle, East Sussex, TN33 0YB, UK
www.hbdi-uk.com

Myers Briggs, Consulting Psychologists Press Inc., 3803 East Bayshore Road, Palo Alto, CA 94303, USA
www.cpp-db.com

Peter Honey Learning, 10 Linden Avenue, Maidenhead, Berks SL6 6HB, UK
www.peterhoneylearning.com

Purple Works, Waltham House, 5-7 St Mary's House, Mill Lane,
Guildford, Surrey, GU1 3TZ, UK
www.purpleworks.com

www.powerupyourmind.com is the website for this book

Index